PORTFOLIO DESIGN

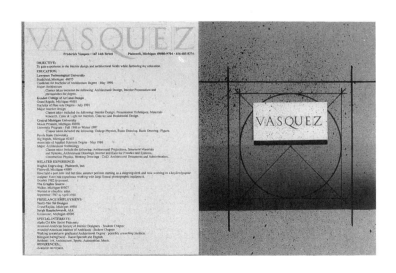
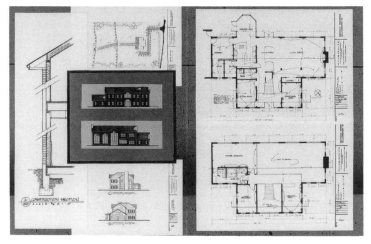
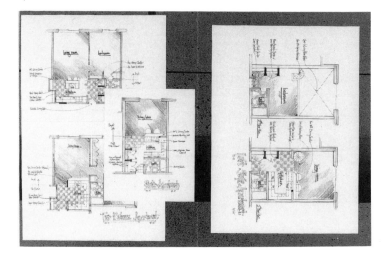

PORTFOLIO DESIGN

Harold Linton

Photographs by Steven Rost

W. W. Norton & Company

New York • London

Copyright © 1996 by Harold Linton

The text of this book is composed in Candida
with the display set in Imago
Manufacturing by Edwards Brothers
Book design by Charlotte Staub
Cover illustration: Andrew R. Tinucci
Photographs on pages 142–145 reprinted with permission
from *Architecture Studio* by Dan Hoffman (Cranbrook
Academy of Art), published by Rizzoli, New York, 1994.

Library of Congress Cataloging-in-Publication Data

Linton, Harold.
    Portfolio design / Harold Linton ; photographs by Steven Rost.
        p. cm.
    "Norton professional book."
    Includes bibliographical references and index.
    ISBN 0-393-73008-5
    1. Architecture—Designs and plans—Presentation drawings.
2. Art portfolios. I. Title.
NA2714.L56 1996
720'.22'2—dc20   96-21653
                                    CIP

ISBN 0-393-73008-5

W. W. Norton & Company, Inc.,
500 Fifth Avenue,
New York NY 10110
http://www.wwnorton.com

W. W. Norton & Company Ltd.,
10 Coptic Street, London WC1A 1PU

0 9 8 7 6 5

To my parents, Ruth and Leonard,
who instilled in their children
an appreciation of and dedication to
a productive life

CONTENTS

FOREWORD

When I look at a design portfolio, I am interested in the content, of course; but I am also interested in the design of the portfolio itself. Sometimes it tells me as much as the work it presents. In it, I can judge the person's eye: the images chosen, how they are placed on a page, how the captions are designed, the choice of type, the color of paper, the design of the cover. I can also tell if the designer is conservative, adventuresome, flashy, restrained, neat, or sloppy.

The portfolio also tells me about the abilities of its designer to communicate ideas and images in graphic form. Much like in a building, there is a great deal of freedom within the physical limits set by the medium and the cultural limits set by convention, and I can tell about the judgment of the designers by how constrained they have been by these limits or by how much freedom they have taken with them. I can even judge how well they have managed their time in either overdoing the portfolio design or in having established an efficient process for preparing it.

Finally, I can see how all of these decisions have come together in a single object; that is, how coherent with the work illustrated is the form in which it is presented, and, just as important, how coherent is the portfolio with regard to the person that it represents. In the design of a portfolio I encounter many of the same issues, problems, skills, and talents that are necessary to produce architecture.

Cesar Pelli

ACKNOWLEDGMENTS

This project could not have happened without the support of many people. I am deeply grateful to Cesar Pelli for his insightful foreword, which reflects an understanding that reaches across both academic and professional experiences.

My friends and colleagues at Lawrence Technological University, who have given freely of their time in support of this work, include: Dr. Charles M. Chambers, President; Dr. Lewis N. Walker, Provost; Dr. Neville H. Clouten, Dean of the College of Architecture and Design; Betty-Lee Seydler-Sweatt, Assistant Dean; Robert Carr, Director of Interior Architecture/Design and Chairman of the Department of Art and Design; Thomas J. Nashlen, Chairman of the Department of

Architecture; William S. Allen, Professor of Architecture and Landscape Design; Thomas Regenbogen, Associate Professor of Architecture; Roy J. Strickfaden, Senior Lecturer in Architectural Illustration; and Nelson Smith and Gretchen Rudy, Lecturers in Architecture.

I am grateful to all of the design students, faculty, and professionals from across the United States, Canada, and Puerto Rico, who gave advice freely and were equally generous in lending their work toward the success of this project.

I also thank Max Underwood, an architect who teaches at Arizona State; David Miller of Miller's Artists Supply, for outstanding graphic production support; Dwayne Reid, Color Detroit Incorporated, for his magic in printing all of the images; Matthew Coates, Studio Assistant; and Ron Church, Studio Assistant.

Special thanks are due to Paul Matelic, a graduate of Lawrence Technical University and Massachusetts Institute of Technology, now of Studiozone, llc. and Warehouse Productions, Inc., for his assistance: the chapter on Digital Portfolios is largely based on information he provided. I am equally indebted to Steven Rost, Associate Professor at Lawrence, who took the photographs for the book and provided the material for the section on photography for portfolios.

Nothing would have been possible, however, without the love of Deeni, Joshua, Jonathan, and Gesso, who helped to make the tough moments as delightful as they can be; and Ruth and Leonard, who instilled in me an appreciation for devotion to work.

INTRODUCTION

This book has been written for students and practitioners of architecture and the environmental design disciplines. Throughout the process of developing the project, I have had the pleasure of corresponding with many university administrators, design professors, and professionals who expressed their overwhelming support for a text about portfolio design for their students and graduates. This project has therefore benefited from the participation of universities from the United States, Canada, and Puerto Rico. More than thirty institutions submitted sample portfolios. I have also benefited from correspondence with the undergraduate, graduate, and postgraduate students whose work is represented here, and who have had recent experience assembling their portfolios for submission to graduate schools or in the pursuit of fellowship and employment opportunities. These students have recently had to undergo the portfolio review process, with all its attendant anxieties, and their work anticipates many of the problems that others will encounter as they learn the basics of portfolio construction and presentation. I have made an attempt to include as many sample pages from these "real world" examples as possible.

The portfolios in this book are, of course, a limited selection of the work being prepared by students of architecture, landscape design, interior design, urban design, and environmental design in nearly two hundred schools in North America. I can make no claim that this book is either complete or even truly representative. However, the student portfolios shown here are those that instructors and heads of department believed to be distinctive and worthy of being shown in this collection, and I believe there are many lessons to be learned from them.

For over a decade, I have been teaching a course entitled Portfolio Design at the College of Architecture and Design at Lawrence Technological University in Southfield, Michigan. The course is a sophomore year requirement for all students of architecture, interior architecture, and architectural illustration. The course serves as an introduction to the practices of portfolio design and how to document one's own work, and it offers students an opportunity to reflect on their accomplishments. It serves our college as an academic review of our students' progress at the conclusion of two years of study and helps to determine their readiness to proceed into upper division course work and to select a program track for the remaining two years of study. The goal of the course is to introduce the concept of the portfolio as a unified and coherent expression of their interests and abilities in architectural design and to impart the discipline of professional preparation and documentation of their work. I have also initiated a senior level elective course entitled Professional Portfolio as a way of capping the students' previous experience and giving them a further opportunity to design and execute a full portfolio for graduate school admissions, employment opportunities, and fellowship and grant proposals.

In teaching these courses I have become aware that many students entering their last years of study or graduating from a four-year degree program do not possess enough exposure to and experience in the portfolio design process. The subject of portfolio design in many architecture schools appears not to be thoroughly addressed. In general, very little graphic evidence has been assembled to demonstrate what portfolios are about, how they are created, and what alternative choices for design are available. In attempting to address this problem I have tried to bring together as many of the existing resources as possible. There are a number of publications devoted to portfolio design for commercial artists, graphic designers, and photographers, and they are listed in the Selected Bibliography. So far as I know, however, there has been no recent effort at summarizing the portfolio design process expressly for students of architecture and the allied disciplines.

During the months of research and contacting various institutions for portfolio samples to include in this book, I realized that many students have widely ranging creative approaches to portfolio preparation, including the design of the enclosing system and all of the samples within. The sample design portfolios gathered here reflect not only energy and commitment but also much talent and creativity. They offer you many insights into today's creative practices of portfolio design, as well as an intriguing look at some innovative forms of enclosure and original strategies for layout and graphic presentation.

It is not my purpose to teach the techniques of cutting, pasting, and binding a portfolio, or the fine points of working with various art materials. Rather, my intention is to present an overview of the practices of portfolio design in architecture and environmental design; to present a variety of current portfolio examples to show the range of graphic possibilities now being explored for the organization and presentation of your work; and to discuss specific technical practices only as they relate to design concepts and the basic principles of portfolio presentation. I hope that the discussions and illustrations will provide you with insight into professional presentation practices that can help to make your work stand out and focus attention on the essential ideas behind that work. The examples have been selected for their clarity and impact. I have tried not to burden the text with technical details but to illustrate a multitude of graphic design alternatives and to show how the most varied strategies can work if informed by an original and creative impulse.

This book also brings together the shared experiences of many leading professionals and educators who have commented on the nature of portfolio practices, helping to make this project especially meaningful. Their willingness to explain the elements of planning, design, typography, binding, computer applications, reproduction processes, and philosophy of presentation is an act of faith that is deeply appreciated. The viewpoints of these designers and educators from across the country only serve to emphasize the importance of creating a strong portfolio.

The role of the portfolio in student and professional presentations has taken on new meaning with the advance of computer technology and digital reprographic systems. The combination of word processing and drawing programs gives even home PC users the equivalent of a complete desktop publishing system and the potential to produce well-designed camera-ready copy. Many architects and designers are now converting their work into digital formats by scanning images into electronic files and manipulating the output to suit their needs. Once in digital format, an image or a design may be altered in fresh and subtle ways, or it may be shown from many views in a simulated three-dimensional environment. A modern architecture portfolio may now include several high-density diskettes, or a CD-ROM, for a full video or multimedia presentation; it may even exist only electronically, on the Internet. For the moment, however, the traditional practices of demonstrating one's abilities in a print format remain strong. After all, draftsmanship and graphic design ability are essential skills for the architect preparing plans. But for the portfolio presentation, the more flexible and higher definition digital imagery of modern scanners and printers will soon challenge traditional print reproduction methods in terms of cost as well as creativity. This book explores some of the new computer techniques as they apply to portfolio design, and some examples are included.

During my two decades of teaching, I have encountered many different kinds of architecture, art, and design students. I have realized that the interests and experiences of young designers can vary widely. Some students do not discover their own talents and abilities until late in their education, while others discover their voice relatively quickly. Some students do not necessarily develop beyond a certain level of self-awareness, while others continue to make strides in all that they do. Design instructors are continually faced with the challenge of "getting through" to a diverse group of students with various levels of ability, commitment, and design experience. We want to give our students "real world exposure," as well as a positive desire to look beyond first impulses and experiment with different formats and possibilities. We also want to communicate the exhilaration associated with the search for one's own identity. Max Underwood, an architect, expresses keen insight into the nature of design education:

The professional training received in architectural schools and professional internships generally focuses upon the transfer of an established body of knowledge necessary for professional competency at a particular moment in time. Within three years after their professional training, many of the facts, skills, and tools that the student-architect learns are obsolete because of the rapid rate of change in contemporary practice. It is at this critical moment that young architects must rely on their education to shape their future professional growth and evolution. The education of individuals must empower them to realize their potential, allowing them to adapt, discover new ideas, and direct their own personal future. Knowledgeable clients seek out the educated architect, rather than the trained architect, to propose answers to the unprecedented conditions of our rapidly changing world. Education must be more than professional training, it must educate the individual, and nurture a trajectory for the lifelong evolution and growth of an individual's talent, mind, and character.

A simple, traditional portfolio layout using a
standard page size and a mixture of photographs,
sketches, elevations, and models mounted on
bristol card stock.
Dieatra Blackburn, North Carolina State
University, Raleigh NC. 11″ x 17″

An Affordable Tradition: Repairing the Urban Fabric

ACSA Affordable Housing Competition

This proposal addresses issues facing a decaying inner city residential neighborhood in a mid-size town. In their present state of disrepair, the small, wood houses characteristic of this area exhibit a rich cultural and architectural heritage. The solution demonstrates respect for this history and contribution to their continued viability through a master plan which restores the density of the existing fabric through the introduction of affordable homes which interpret the existing architectural vocabulary. Both the master plan and the individual houses provide an architectural framework which enhances the physical and visual physical activity of the street vital in this area.

The project master plan and the form of the homes are derived from extensive site analysis and study of the local vernacular. Each house is sixteen feet wide and forty feet long with a corridor on one side linking the living spaces. The upper floor of the house is left unfinished and is intended to accommodate growing families. The front porch is an important extension of the home, a bridge between the individual and the community.

The proposal won first place in a national competition co-sponsored by the American Collegiate Schools of Architecture.

1.
What Is the
Design Portfolio?

Your portfolio is simply a collection of your best pieces of design work, arranged in such a way as to show your interests and talents as an architect or a designer, and the growth of those interests and talents over the course of your education and professional career. Since buildings, landscape designs, and interiors, or even models of them, are impractical to transport, you use a portfolio instead. It showcases your accomplishments in the graphic form of text and illustrations, and it is usually enclosed in some kind of binder or case for protection and easy handling. A finely tailored portfolio is the most important tool you can bring to an application for admission to graduate school or a design grant or competition or to a job interview or to a potential client. In the course of your career, you will probably have to prepare many portfolios, each one adapted to one of these different purposes. In each case, your portfolio needs immediate and dramatic impact to distinguish you from others with whom you are competing, and it has to clearly answer the questions in the minds of those reviewing your work, for whatever purpose. The portfolio is a graphic history of your skills and accomplishments, and it must be seen not only as a problem in design, but as a tool to promote yourself to prospective employers and clients. Each year more and more architecture and design students enter the job market, and the competition grows more intense.

The challenge of proper self-promotion through portfolio design is to be able to objectively assess your strengths and accomplishments. Preparing a portfolio requires you to take a step back from your own design work and to make an evaluation as unemotionally as possible. Learning to be observant about the strengths and weaknesses of your work encourages the development of a critical and unbiased eye useful to the portfolio design process and to your professional career generally. Inviting the opinions of trusted advisors and colleagues also helps to eliminate the initial fears you may have about putting together a portfolio. Planning a portfolio presentation also requires a keen sense of organization and an ability to arrange various written and visual materials

I always want to see examples of a job applicant's work from every step of the design process, including doodles, thumbnail sketches, renderings, everything. I want to get an idea of what it would be like to work with the applicant throughout a project. The final renderings are actually the least important part of the portfolio to me because they don't show the process.

**Bryan Gailey, Vice President and Principal
SDI-HTI
New York, N. Y.**

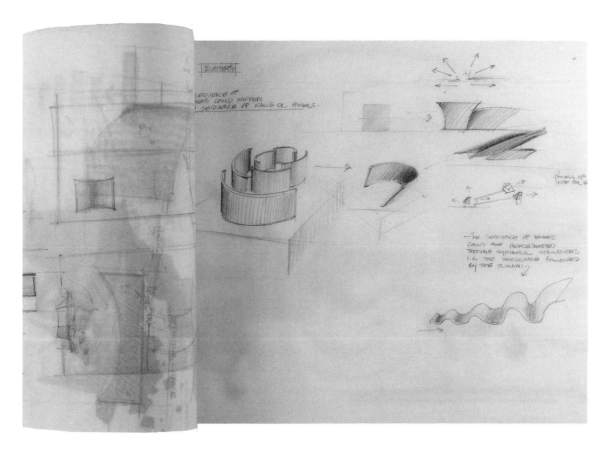

An elegant and imaginatively packaged portfolio. The enclosing system consists of a series of individual wood-laminated binders with vellum pages. The contents include conceptual sketches, drawings, photographs, and renderings.
Armen Savada Gharabegian, Art Center College of Design, Pasadena CA. 14" x 10 1/2"

into a unified graphic package, as well as the ability to maintain a focused vision throughout the development of the presentation. Those who review your portfolio will be looking for a businesslike attitude and a pragmatic "soundness" in your work, as well as creativity and pure grace and beauty. Creativity is important, but employers want designers able to solve problems economically and quickly. As an architect, environmental or interior designer, you are proposing to spend other people's money, a lot of it, and a solid portfolio presentation will go a long way toward persuading others that you can be trusted with that responsibility.

Student designers with a creative future will have a natural curiosity about life and the world. Assembling a portfolio is an exercise that prepares you for future accomplish-

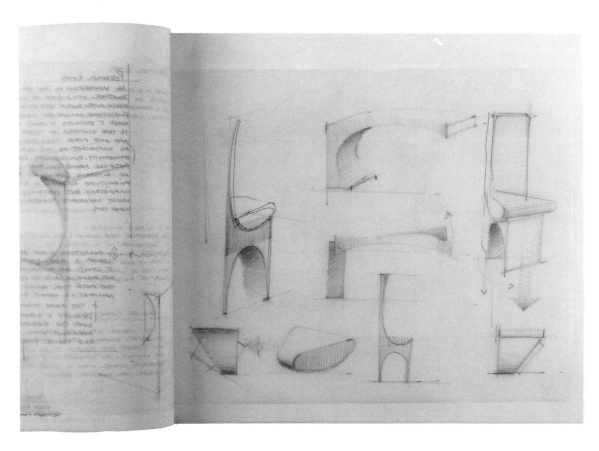

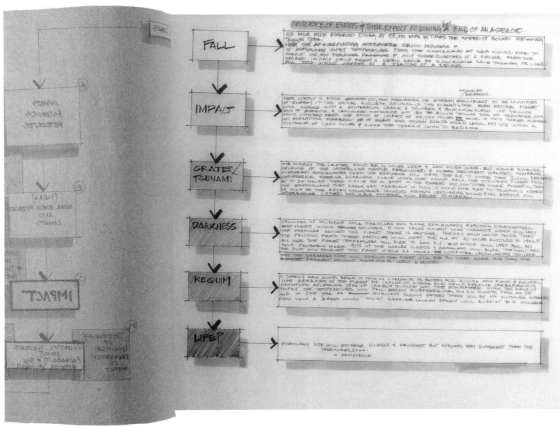

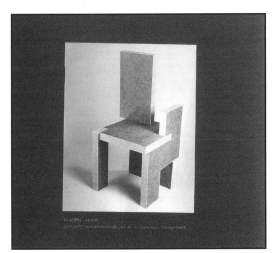

ment in the real world by teaching how to evaluate your own work, and to understand how that work will appear to other professionals. A good portfolio illustrates your strengths and demonstrates that you have a clear understanding of format, graphic design, typography, concept development, problem-solving, and business communication. Your portfolio not only represents a body of work acquired throughout academic and professional life, but it displays this work in such a way that your design philosophy is made manifest. Of course, most undergraduate students have not chosen a specific area of design, nor perhaps developed a design philosophy, and tend to be generalists. This is not a drawback, because many good designers are generalists; they can solve any problem. Having a focus too early in your career can limit possibilities for growth and development. Your portfolio represents an evolution, not an end in itself. The educational experience involves growth, and growth often requires you to set aside prior knowledge to consider new concepts and directions. As Max Underwood says:

Great portfolios assist in our understanding of not only individual designers and their work, but their larger design vision and contributions in allowing us to see our world anew. One recalls the story of the arrival of Frank Lloyd Wright's Wasmuth portfolio in Peter Behrens' office, and work stopping for the rest of the day as the office staff of Le Corbusier, Mies van der Rohe, Walter Gropius, et al. leafed through the pages and saw their modern world anew. . . . A

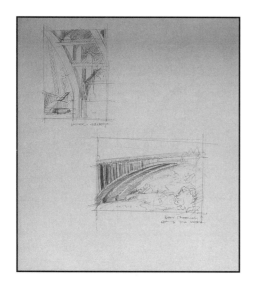

quality portfolio is like a garden, constantly being watered for future nourishment and beauty.

There is no single formula for assembling a good portfolio. Not only will the thinking of architects and designers change in the course of their career, but portfolio objectives change. In applying for advanced study or a professional position, the goal may be to demonstrate a variety of interests, or a process of growth and learning over time. In applying for a specific grant or competition, the goal may be to demonstrate knowledge and expertise in a specialized area known to be of interest to the grant or competition administrators. Some professional portfolios are prepared only after considerable consultation with a client, and present the designer's ideas about how a single project might be carried out, complete with a specific cost analysis. How focused the portfolio presentation is often depends upon what the recipient is looking for. Remember, you are selling yourself, or your ability to execute a particular project or work in a particular environment. You will want to demonstrate ingenuity and uniqueness to make a strong impression, but you must also demonstrate sound judgment.

An effective portfolio presentation may be the only means of getting your foot in the door. Most professionals prefer to review an applicant's portfolio before scheduling a meeting. You drop off or send the portfolio to the reviewers before an interview, so it makes the all-important first impression. It

must show everything that you want to show clearly and dramatically. It must be self-explanatory, and it must anticipate the concerns of the reviewers. The portfolio, as I have said, is a form of self-promotion, and as with any good sales presentation, knowing what the clients are looking for is the best preparation. Preparing a portfolio for a position with a particular architecture firm would certainly involve researching that firm's previous projects and its niche in the marketplace.

The pieces you select for inclusion in your portfolio should demonstrate your interest and aptitude for serious education in architecture and the related design disciplines. For a general presentation of your abilities, the works you select should show diversity in design experience, in the subject matter chosen for exploration, in the variety of mediums employed, as well as communication skills and conceptual abilities. There are many different elements to consider and many decisions to be made in preparing a portfolio. Following is a summary of the key considerations to which you will be introduced in this book.

We will, first of all, talk about the need to establish habits of *documenting* your work from the beginning of your career, and the need to develop skills in photography to keep a record of your work. A basic course in photography is highly recommended for every student of architecture and the allied disciplines, and a part of the time you devote to any project should be devoted to preparing materials for others to see it.

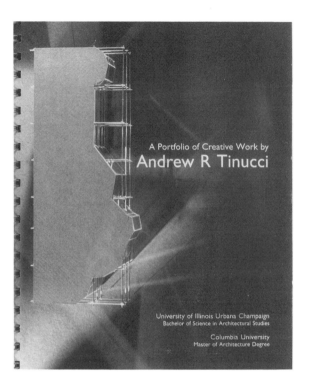

Cover and an interior spread of a portfolio with dramatic sepia-toned photographs. The format is a standard photographic size.
Andrew R. Tinucci, University of Illinois, Champaign-Urbana IL. 8″ x 10″

We will then review the *objectives* of the portfolio. What is included in a portfolio largely depends, as I have said, on the audience it is intended for, and what you want to say to that audience about your work. What skills do you want to emphasize, what areas do you enjoy working in, how do you want to focus your interests in the future? You have limited space and reviewers have limited time, and you want them to see quickly and clearly what they are looking for in a potential employee or graduate student .

The objective guides the *portfolio audit*, the next step in the process. Here you select the projects for inclusion and do some basic editing, that is, decide how many pages of the portfolio should be devoted to each project, which pieces of work should represent the project and which should be excluded, what type of reproduction method would be appropriate for each piece, and what should

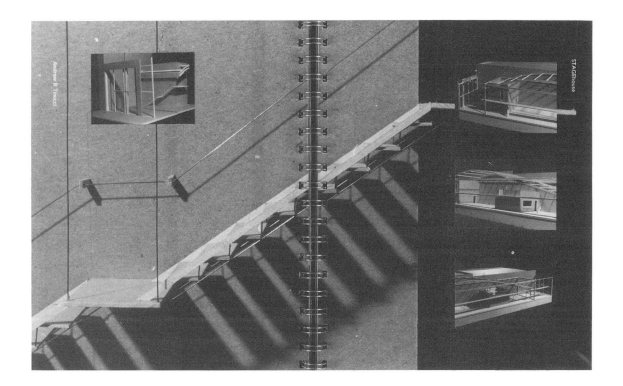

be the order of the projects within the portfolio. Remember that no amount of beautiful photography or packaging can make up for second-rate material. By this time you have developed some ability to pass judgment on whether or not a particular project has been executed skillfully, and it goes without saying that you should not include projects that you are dissatisfied with. But it is also important to make certain that the work included is your work rather than the work of a team (or that your part in the project is accurately described), and that the projects bear some relationship to the kinds of skills you wish to advertise, whether that be site planning, interior design, graphics skills, or draftsmanship.

The next step is to decide upon the general *format* of the portfolio. The format is defined as the size and shape of the portfolio and its pages, and is determined by judgments made

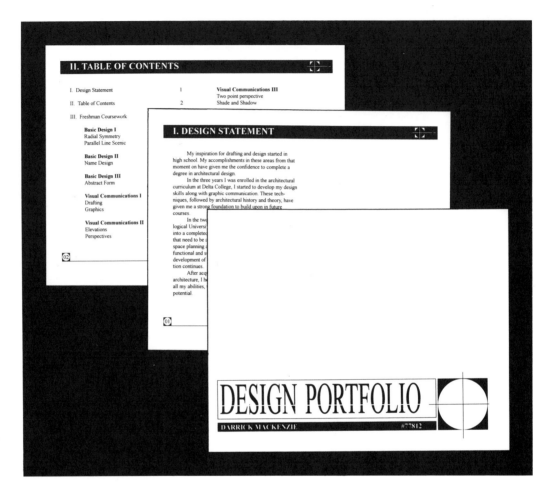

Graphic design studies of opening
page sequences from a sophomore
portfolio class. The elements include
cover, table of contents, design statement, and index.
The format is 11"x 8 ½".
Darrick Mackenzie,
Lawrence Technological University,
Southfield MI.

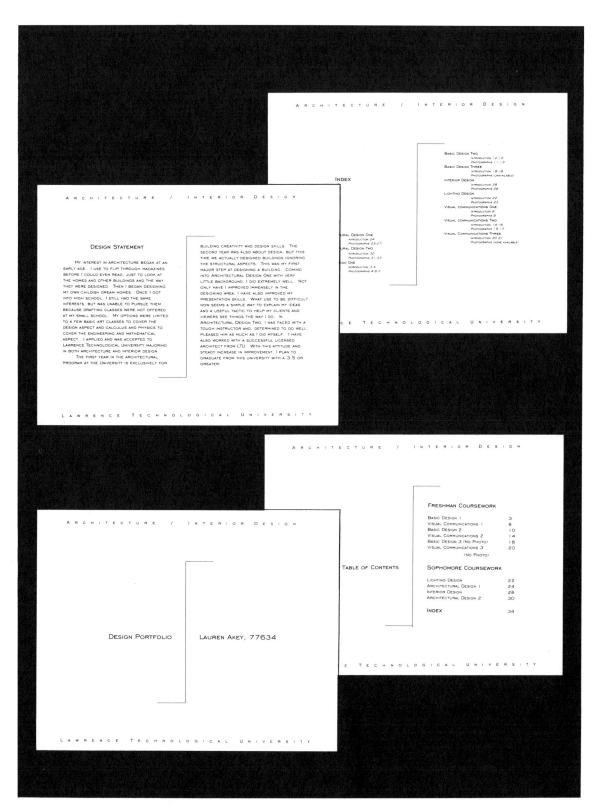

Lauren Akey, Lawrence Technological University, Southfield MI.

A portfolio is, in many ways, a kind of window that opens up, not just the work of the student, but their manner of thinking. The way in which the material is presented, the evidence of a concern for the crafting of each element, suggests volumes about the character of the person who puts it together. An articulate, concise, and consciously crafted portfolio, even one which conveys unspectacular work, sets up concrete expectations about the student's thoroughness and attention to detail. These are the qualities most employers are seeking in an entry level architectural intern.

Roger Spears
Assistant Professor of Architecture
School of Design
North Carolina State University

during the portfolio audit about the best way to present the projects you have chosen. The format may be vertical (or portrait), in which the pages have greater height than width, or horizontal (or landscape), in which the width is greater than the height, or square. It may be a standard size or oversize or a mini-portfolio. Within the broad concept of format, you have to select a specific page size, so the discussion of format will lead to a discussion of paper and board sizes and types, and folding and mounting processes.

Once the size and construction of the pages is decided, we come to the question of the *enclosing system*. The enclosing system is the physical means by which the contents of the portfolio is stored and protected. It may be a commercial leather or vinyl folder with or without a loose-leaf or spiral binding mechanism, or a customized case made of cardboard, wood, metal, or another material. Pages may be bound (attached to one another or the binding) or unbound (loose) sheets or boards. Unbound pages (plates) may get out of order and can be damaged more easily when handled, though they are ideal if you are making a presentation in person, so you can hold them up for more than one person to view at a time. Many professionals consider a zippered folder with a ring-binding system to be the most practical choice if the portfolio is meant to circulate among many people and remain out of the designer's hands for some time. Some binders feature collapsible stands that fold out into little portable easels for page display.

Of course, the enclosing system today could even be a small plastic box containing computer diskettes, or the diskettes might be included as part of a more conventional presentation. Whatever enclosing system you choose, the reviewer must be able to manipulate it easily and work his or her way through the presentation in a simple, straightforward manner.

From these basic decisions about form and size and content, we will move on to the complex subjects of *graphic design* and *page layout*. Graphic design refers to how we translate architectural concepts into easily understood terms on the printed page. Remember that the portfolio depends upon visual images to get its message across. In effect, its function is to tell a story without words, or with as few words as possible. You must now learn to think of structures not in terms of how they will stand on real sites, but how they will present themselves on the flat page, and how much of their ingenuity and complexity will be visible through different types of graphic—that is, printed (two-dimensional)—media. Does the layout make it easier to visualize the structures portrayed? Or conversely, does the design get in the way of seeing what is on the page? Does the form suit the content? Think of two magazines of the same size that have different designs to appeal to different readerships. The readers of *Time* magazine would probably object to having to digest their news in the graphic form of *Wired*. Graphic design involves subtle matters of cultural convention and human

A boxed edition of plates large enough to accommodate various types of documentation,
including photographs, printed text on transparent overlays, and double- and triple-folded
panels.
Brita Brookes, University of Michigan,
Ann Arbor MI. 9″ x 12″

psychology. Why are the most important
news stories to be found in the right-hand
columns of a newspaper? What attracts the
eye to certain colors or shapes? And how
successfully can we violate these conventions
to achieve a new effect? Graphic thinking
involves decisions about placement of text
and typography, size, placement, and distrib-
ution of illustrations, and choice of reproduction method. These may be new and
unfamiliar areas for students used to conceiv-
ing of form in three dimensions.

Page layout is a vast subject in its own

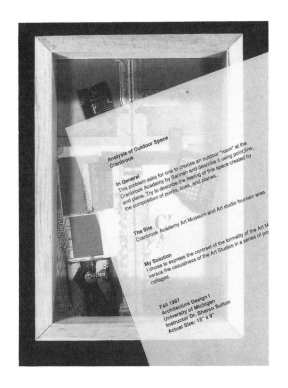

right, always evolving, and we can only cover some basic principles in this book. We will discuss the creation of a *grid*, an underlying structure or template that guides you in positioning and scaling images and text while helping to maintain a consistent design. You should study examples of page design in current books and periodicals on architecture, graphic design, and related subjects to survey the trends that are in practice today. One of your responsibilities as a designer is to keep up with what is new and maintain a broad knowledge of new work in the field. You cannot create out of abstractions; you must expose yourself to the work of others, absorb the graphic ideas of the design community as a whole, and build upon them.

Page design is also affected by decisions about methods of reproduction made during the portfolio audit. Depending upon the documentation available to you, you will have decided how a particular piece of work should be reproduced—through original art, offset printing, photocopying, or photography. Architectural plans, sketches, and simple drawings can be effectively reproduced through a variety of simple methods, from photocopying to photostats, in positive or negative form. But complex drawings, graphics using more than one medium, collages involving the layering of drawings, and three-dimensional models are best handled through photographic processes and even offset printing. The nature of the material you can draw upon may suggest a particular page design

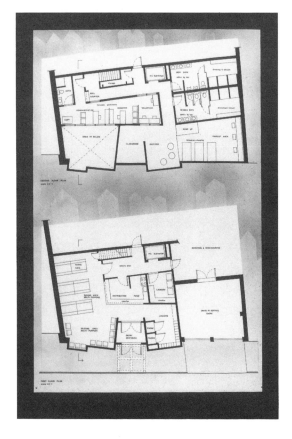

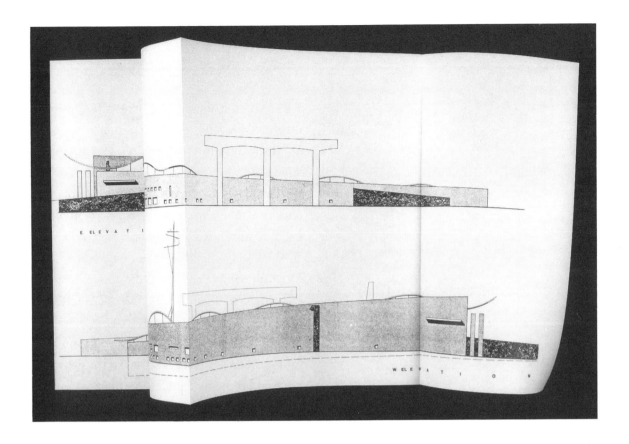

strategy because of its shape, its style, its detail, the strength of contrasting tones in graphic images, or some other quality.

You must then consider text and captions, for these elements bring out features of your work that may not be obvious when a viewer looks at the graphic elements. To organize the material selected, you may have a title page, a table of contents, a page numbering system (especially important with a series of unbound plates), and even an index. The goal, of course, is to make the portfolio easier for the reviewer to comprehend.

After graphic design and page layout, we will discuss the subtle matter of *sequencing*. You have already decided upon the number and general order of projects during the portfolio audit, but what is the best way to arrange the pages or plates within each pro-

ject, and how should you handle the transitions between projects? Sequencing is equivalent to editing in filmmaking, and concerns
itself with how one thing follows another in a
continuous or disconnected series of images,
and how much space or "weight" is given to
each element. A sequence may be governed
by the changing size of the images or their
growing complexity, evolving forms, or a
change of scale or perspective. Sequencing is
the process of deciding how many pages to
devote to each project, how to build interest
in the project, and how to make transitions
between projects and yet maintain a consistent design.

To illustrate some of these basic concepts,
let's take a look at several quite different
approaches to portfolio design.

Armen S. Gharabegian, an Environmental
Design student, presented his work in a ser-
ries of individual wood-laminated binders
containing vellum pages (pages 23–27). The
portfolio emphasizes drawing and design
process, with notes, research, methodology,
and design development.

Architecture student Dieatra Blackburn
prepared her portfolio in application for a
traveling fellowship from Skidmore, Owings
& Merrill. She focused on the problem of
housing the homeless in hospices and private
homes (pages 20–21). The portfolio consisted
of unbound sheets of bristol board with photographs and text mounted directly on the
board surface. Page numbers were clearly
lettered on the reverse side of each plate, and
the entire suite was placed into a ready-

made box intended for archival photographs (not shown). Working with a page size of 11" x 17," set by SOM, Dieatra used an invisible grid to position the elements of each page in solid blocklike form. Negative space is used as effectively as printed space. This open area directs the eye toward the images, giving them importance beyond what their size would indicate. The use of negative space as a design element, with the images reduced and offset on the page, lends a quality of asymmetry and understatement that is very effective.

Andrew R. Tinucci's portfolio submission (pages 28–29) for a graduate program used a wire-bound format with sepia-toned prints adhered to the page surfaces. The double-page spread shows how he extended the design across the "gutter" (inner margins) of the portfolio. An interesting contrast is created through photomontage by using smaller photographs of details inset on the full-page images.

These portfolios reflect careful planning and forethought about how the portfolio will work as a whole. In the same way that animators and filmmakers storyboard their work before production, these students gave a great deal of attention to their over-all designs to solve as many problems as possible before actually assembling their presentations.

The design process and the various steps described above are meant to help you pre-plan as many important elements as possible. The ability, so to speak, to see the finished

The portfolio is an important tool in every phase of our program. Students are required to prepare a portfolio of work completed in each studio from design fundamentals through thesis. Each studio instructor submits a portfolio of student work documenting each semester's results. Portfolios are required for admission into the five-year Bachelor of Architecture degree program. Portfolios form an essential component of virtually every decision I make.

Jonathan Friedman, Dean
School of Architecture
New York Institute of Technology

Design projects:

1) Brucke Park was an urban 'air-rights' project over a major interstate highway in Columbus, Ohio. The design solution addressed the connection between a historic brewery district to the south and the modern high-rise buildings to the north.

2) Greenus Loci proposed a sustainable historic community in which integration of energy-efficient systems, urban agronomy, and active social interaction increased quality of life and a state of balance.

3) The residential project, including the working drawing, was a typical example of an exercise required to be completed within two hours.

4) The sorority design was a brief project illustrating the potential of a property considered for purchase.

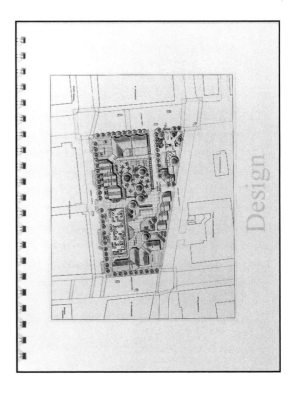

From the graduate portfolio of a land-scape architecture student, these pages show strength in draftsmanship and sketching, and dramatic page design.
Elizabeth C. Saunders,
The Ohio State University,
Columbus OH. 8 1/2″ x 11″

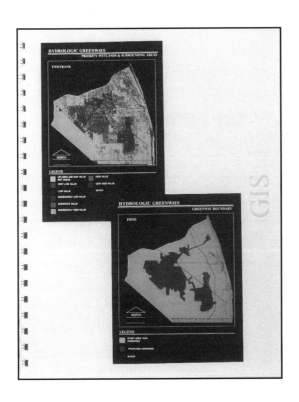

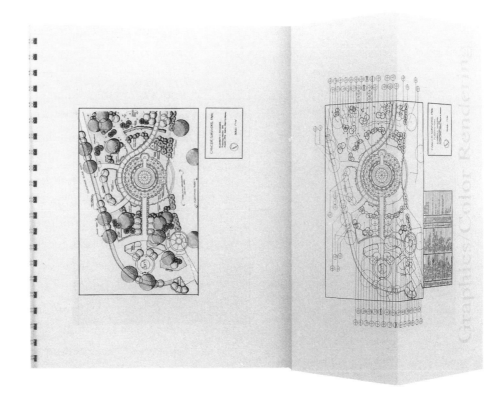

One of the most interesting aspects of our pro-
fession of architecture is that it is tangible.
Drawings, models, and simulations are not only
tools but artistic creations as well. A thought-
fully planned and skillfully executed portfolio is
the best evidence of an individual's competence,
skill, and talent. In evaluating future
performance in academic or professional design
activity, the portfolio remains the single most
informative device.

> Romolo Martemucci, AIA
> Interim Department Head, Architecture
>   Department
> Pennsylvania State University

sculpture inside the block of stone before the
chisel is taken up saves enormous time and
effort, and indicates both organization and
creativity.

The illustrations on pages 30–31 are
graphic design studies for my sophomore
portfolio course. These pages were produced
on a computer and illustrate a variety of successful type treatments for a portfolio. They
all include a design statement, which may
simply summarize the student's developing
interest in the field of architecture or define
the approach to a particular project. A table
of contents and index provide a way for the
reviewer to navigate within the portfolio and
locate subjects of particular interest. The
computer desktop publishing system makes a
great many styles and sizes of type available
to the designer. In these samples the type has
not been overdesigned; there is a pleasing
sense of unity between text and heads and
other elements. Whether the students chose
single or double-spaced text, justified or un-
justified lines, upper- or lowercase initial
caps, or normal or boldface type, they produced effective design through the intelligent
combination of elements.

The portfolio of Brita Brookes (pages 34–37)
illustrates the full range of creative techniques, design influences, and production
processes that can be brought into play. She
created three identical boxed sets of plates as
part of a successful application to graduate
school. The container is made of wood and
the sliding lid is treated as a surface for collage portraiture. A wide variety of materials

demonstrate the range of the designer's abilities, including assemblage and photocollage, sketching, modeling, and drafting. All of the work is mounted on solid core black mat board as individual plates. Ms. Brookes created several three-dimensional constructions that were carefully illuminated, photographed, color-copied, and then mounted. Project statements were printed on translucent paper and included at selected points within the sequence of plates. Several pages with larger drawings were carefully sized to work as two-panel or three-panel foldouts. The size of the black mounting board is constant and permits changes in the size of the paper for individual presentations. This portfolio brings together different elements in a coordinated graphic package, and clearly reveals the designer's style, personal tastes, and professional interests.

Sample pages from a portfolio in landscape architecture by Elizabeth Saunders are shown on pages 40–41. The presentation includes computer graphics, color rendering, and freehand drawing. Each section is identified by a heading, beginning with dark type that is screened down to a softer gray tint on successive pages. Because she needed additional space, she used fold-out panels for her landscape plans.

Frederick Vasquez's interior design portfolio (pages 44–46) shows his well-developed drafting abilities, essential for this specialty. The enclosing system is a simple corrugated cardboard box, with the work contained in folders, each with a hand-lettered title. Most

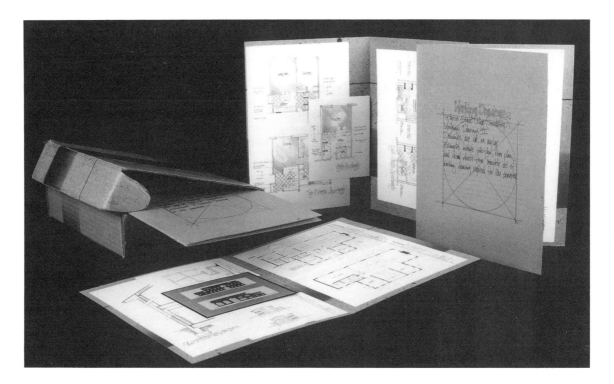

A corrugated cardboard box and folders of
speckled paper with hand-lettered titles make
simple but effective packaging for this interior
design student's application to graduate school.
Frederick Vasquez,
Lawrence Technological University,
Southfield MI. 8 1/2″ x 11″

of the reproduction work was done on photo-
copiers. The black-and-white photographs
were reproduced on a color copier because
the printing inks for color copies give a very
dense effect and capture the subtleties of rich
blacks and grays better than a black-and-
white copier.

Finally, let's look at the portfolio of a professional, Professor Mike Haverland of Yale
University (pages 48–49). A good example of
thorough documentation, these pages
demonstrate the evolution and growth that
transpires during and after a designer's formal education. Each project begins with an
introductory page explaining the goals of the
work, and features a bold black space
instead of an opening illustration. Well-
lighted models are expertly photographed
and shown in a sequence from smaller views
to larger views. Drawings are carefully com-

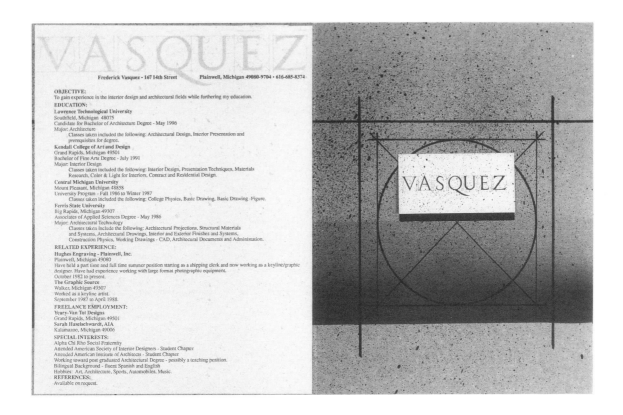

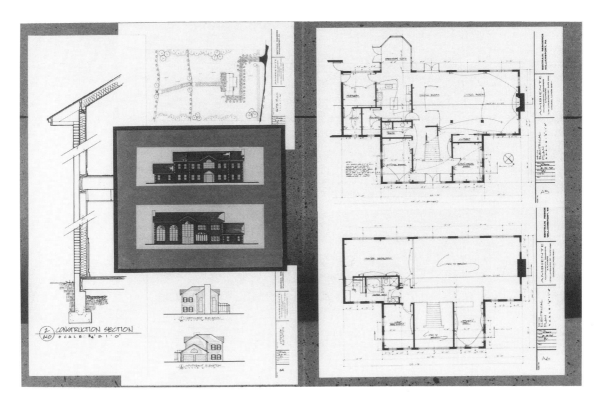

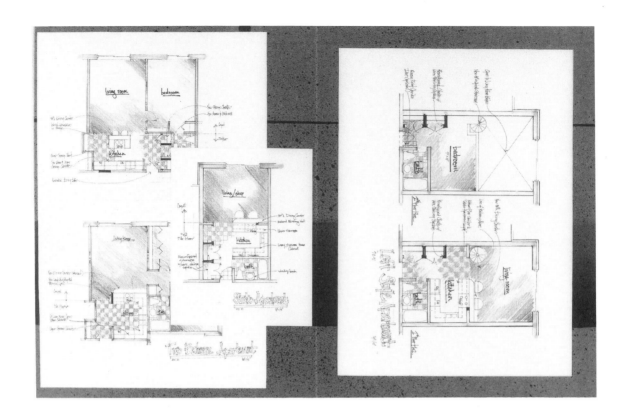

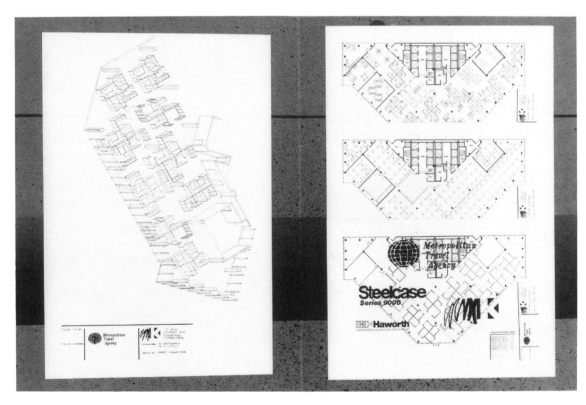

posed and reproduced in crisp, clean black line on white paper.

A good portfolio also requires good writing skills as well as design ability, often the hardest element for visual people. You must demonstrate your ability to articulate in written form what your goals are. You must be able to write clear proposals and analyses of projects, as well as illustrate them. While the images carry the greatest weight, written communication is an essential business skill that must supplement your design abilities.

If you are enthusiastic about your work, you will find portfolio assembly an intriguing and creative activity. But it also involves hard judgments. You must act like an editor as well as a creator. You must get your point across with a limited number of images, demonstrating your ability to be selective and critical. Every page or plate must build on the previous page by adding new ideas without redundancy, by expanding concepts, by taking a fresh approach to how the material is presented. You will then have a portfolio that sets you apart from the many others who are competing for the same job or academic program.

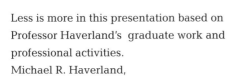

Fish Hatchery; Processing Plant

Site, Context and Process	Critic: Turner Brooks
Yale University: First Year, Spring 1993	Three weeks, five weeks

Fresh Water Fish Hatchery and Fishermen's Cabin; Vermont: This project attempts to develop a language appropriate for this "type", a fish hatchery, in its New England context. A breeding raceway connects two points of a local stream to provide natural water flow while creating a large scale gesture on the landscape. The hatchery's form is based on the contours of the hill, vernacular clerestory lighting, and the program requirements. The temperature control system is a concrete tower which combines well water, spring water and stream water. An office for the manager connects these for monitoring while also viewing down the raceway. Fishermen's cabins lie on the stream yet have a clear relationship to the artificial stream, the raceway. Fishermen and visitors ride carts which also carry supplies and mature fish to the end of the raceway for transport to the main processing plant in Maine.

Fish Processing Plant, Aquarium and Research Facility; Rockland, Maine: This project consists of two relatively modest sheds, a processing plant and research facility, all along an existing bank of rubble and stone at the water's edge near large warehouses and factories. The entire site is a workyard and is part of the process. The aquarium becomes not a small room for viewing fish but rather transforms the entire site into a museum to view this process through the experiential promenade; it facilitates the change in elevation, affords connection to the water and so the sheds. Spaces and structures throughout the site, including the office space interventions as well as the aquarium cases, are objectified and articulated to be analogous to museum cases and artifacts. A small scale fish hatchery also exists as an isolated object for research and exhibition.

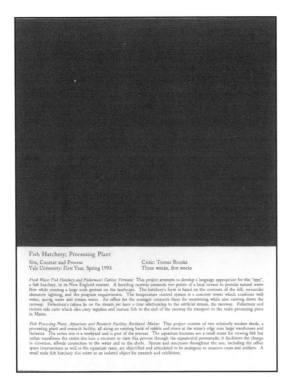

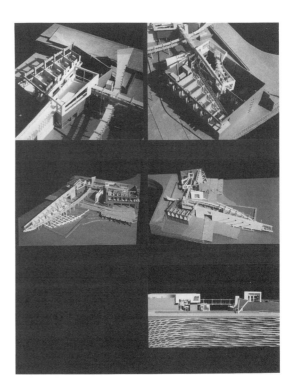

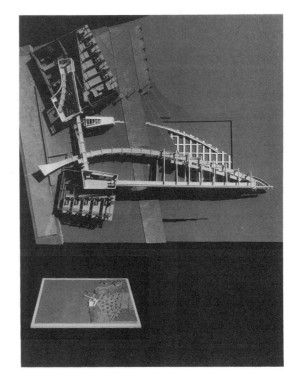

Less is more in this presentation based on
Professor Haverland's graduate work and
professional activities.
Michael R. Haverland,
Yale University, New Haven CT. 8 1/2" x 11"

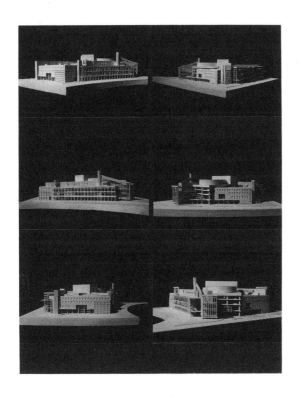

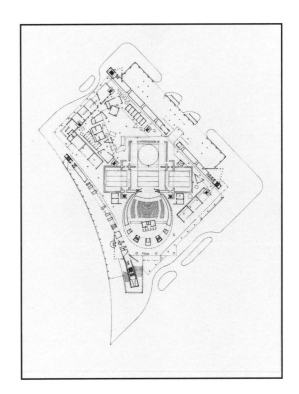

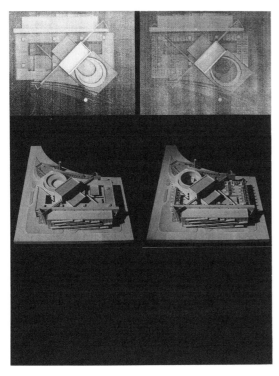

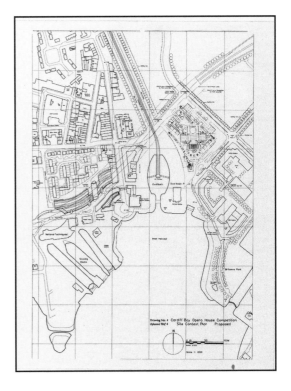

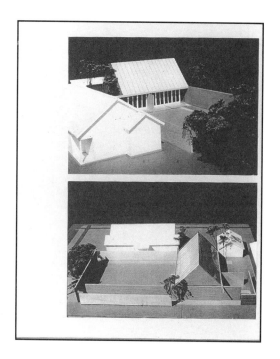

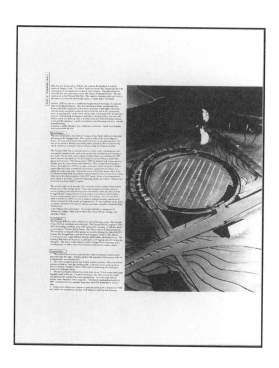

Professor Reese used indoor and outdoor photography and graphics in these pages from his professional portfolio.
Professor John Reese, University of Illinois, Champaign-Urbana IL. 8 1/2" x 11"

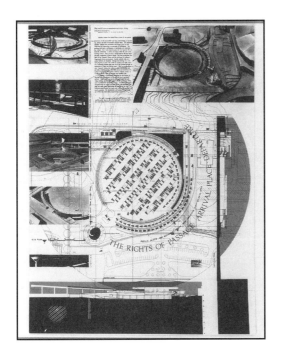

2.
Getting Started

The process of designing a portfolio really starts at the beginning of your career as a design student, when you complete your first renderings or site plans or models. If you are just now considering assembling a portfolio, having given no prior thought to the matter, it is a little late to discover this, and you will have to take action to catch up, but the first rule of portfolio preparation is to record your work—all your work—at all stages and from all perspectives, and carefully preserve that record. Obviously, you cannot prepare a portfolio if you do not have at your disposal a considerable quantity of artwork representing what you have done. Get in the habit of pho-

Documentation of student work should begin
very early in their academic career. Even though
much of this work will eventually be edited and
replaced, it is important to make those initial
steps to record, photograph, and create the com-
position. Each successive update becomes more
sophisticated. Drawings may be included if they
clearly reflect the final design. The text should
be clear, concise, and consistent in format.

Elizabeth J. Louden
Assistant Professor of Architecture
Texas Technological University

tographing or making copies of your work
through some other reprographic process
from the beginning of your career, before, as
will happen over time, those projects are lost,
disassembled, given away, or become dog-
eared. This cannot be urged upon you often
enough by your instructors, and it's a lesson
you must never forget. You cannot judge now
what might be important for inclusion in a
portfolio three or five years ahead, and documents that have disappeared or been
destroyed or creased and smudged—documents for which no copies have been made—
are useless to you.

Most two-dimensional design evidence in
architecture and related design studio
coursework is created on traditional supports
such as illustration, mat and foam-core
boards, mylar, and vellum at a size ranging
from 18" x 24" to 20" x 30"; the output from
plotters may be even larger. Because, for
portability, portfolios are typically smaller in
size than the original work, you need to select an appropriate method for reproduction,
and usually, reduction. The three most common methods of reproduction for two-dimensional work are photography, photostats, and
photocopies. The choice of method will depend partly on the nature of the original
work and partly on economics (professional
photography is expensive).

Photocopy original black and white two-
dimensional work and text material; a range
of colored papers, card stocks, transparent,
translucent, and acetate sheets is available in
standard sizes (8 1/2" x 11", 8 1/2" x 14", 11"

x 17"). Large-format copy machines (over 11" x 17") are available in copy centers and companies that specialize in printing architectural and engineering drawings. You can photocopy on large sheets of mylar, vellum, and even illustration and mat board, or reduce the artwork in one or two steps to normal portfolio size.

Good photocopies and photostats are appropriate for work with a great deal of detail, such as construction documents, but be careful not to reduce the work so severely that the notes and dimensions become illegible. Original two-dimensional work created in black and white with high contrast can be photostatted or photocopied, in positive or negative. Original work with limited and very distinctive gray tones may also be statted or photocopied with a line screen.

Original two-dimensional work and all three-dimensional work (models) with values of gray (shading) must be photographed to retain tone—and in color, if color is to be reproduced. Many students use color copiers, and the quality has improved dramatically in recent years. Bubble-jet printers produce creditable reproductions, but color photographs remain sharper in image resolution and color fidelity.

As use of the computer in design spreads, archiving of work done electronically, both student and professional, is becoming more a matter of course. But most students do not work exclusively on the computer—and even if they did, graphics consume a great deal of memory. So for the present, remember con-

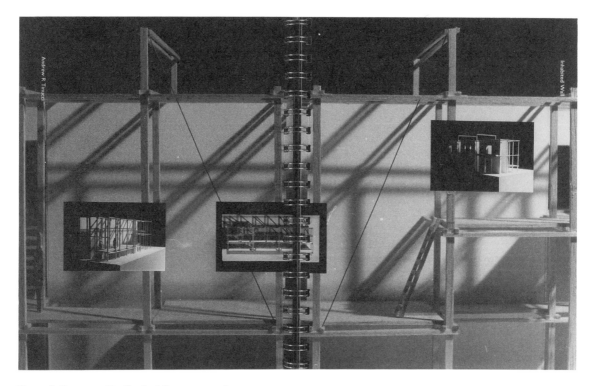

Though the overall effect of these pages is
strongly photographic, architectural plans make
a good foil for the dramatically lighted models.
Andrew R. Tinucci, University of Illinois,
Champaign-Urbana IL. 8" x 10"

tinually to record your work in progress and
retain every sketch. Get in the habit early on
of reproducing all your work during the
process of creation and upon completion.
Models and constructions deteriorate over
time or are lost, and drawings and site plans
are difficult to preserve in pristine condition.
If possible, record your work while it is still
fresh, and keep more than one copy. Don't
discard your preliminary drawings: a selection of them belongs in your portfolio. Such
drawings convey your ability at problem-
solving, a skill that is more valuable to design
firms than a perfectly turned out portfolio
showing only finished work.

The need to record your work raises an
important consideration: how should you get
it photographed? Some students use the photographic services housed in their university
or college—these may be professional, a
work-study student setup, or a student-run

operation. Professional photographers offer photographic and copy-stand services in most cities; they are listed in the Yellow Pages. Always ask for references, prices, and samples before you retain the services of a professional.

Even if you have your work photographed professionally, a working knowledge of photography and reprographic techniques is essential for any design student, and must be acquired fairly quickly after you begin professional study. Even if you are only ordering photographs, knowing how a 35mm camera or a larger-format camera works, being familiar with digital photography, and understanding the photostat process will serve you well. If your photographs are made by a commercial studio, you must be familiar with the terminology of photography so you can give clear instructions to the photographer. Photographic literacy will eliminate misunderstandings and reduce your costs.

Your understanding of the principles of photography must be thorough, for your work is not simply being photographed, but being photographed in ways that should make its virtues clear to those who are unfamiliar with it. It is beyond the scope of this book to delve into the technical issues of photography, but whether you are planning to take your own photographs or to supervise photography, a basic photography class is highly recommended, and advanced courses are desirable. The camera does not see like the human eye, and it takes considerable experience to understand how it will interpret light. The first efforts trying to photograph colored objects or landscapes with a roll of black-and-white film will reveal that the camera gives different "weights" to colors than does the eye because it records values without the influence of hues.

The best portfolio photography is done under studio conditions, with controlled lighting, with the camera held in a fixed position by a tripod, giving great flexibility in exposure times, depth of field, and perspective. Under such conditions, at least the photographer can be reasonably certain that the mistakes are his or her own.

The quality of photographic presentation in a portfolio is determined by several factors. It is essential, first of all, that the model, drawing, or item to be photographed be intelligently crafted and appropriate for inclusion. Photography flattens three-dimensional objects, and it takes some experimentation to see what happens to them when they are represented in two dimensions. While it is rare that a good photograph can make a poorly crafted work look good, a poor photograph can surely undermine the quality of a fine piece of work. The photograph must be sharp and reveal details, and must show the care that has been taken in designing the work. The biggest problem is controlling light and achieving proper illumination, best done in a photo studio. Large, flat pieces of artwork must be placed on a copy stand and photographed dead on, perfectly perpendicular, if they are not to be distorted and appear trapezoidal in shape. Models require a con-

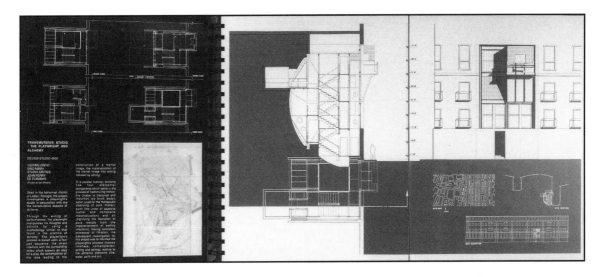

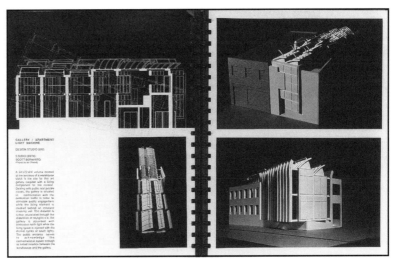

Positive and negative photostats and photographs make strong graphics.
Ian Scott Sheard, University of Houston, Houston TX. 8 1/2" x 11"

trasting background because the materials they are made from rarely photograph with the strong contrasts of black and white art. Good photography requires you to make decisions about light and shadow, texture, depth of field (what is in or out of focus), and scale. Light can be manipulated so that shadows emphasize the geometry of the structure. Take details from photographs and enlarge them to make them clearer; lay the blow-ups over or next to the main image.

Though photographs or reproductions should be made as you are working on the projects, the decision about which views to include and how to position and crop them will be made in tandem with design and layout decisions during the process of preparing the portfolio, so that the whole page design makes sense.

The choice of photographic paper also offers many alternatives. A print can be made on warm- or cold-toned paper, on sepia-toned paper, or the print may be hand-colored with paints or pencils. Photographs can be mounted on white, black, or colored stock, with glossy, matte, pearl, or textured surfaces. Well-mounted photographs—whether adhered by dry mounting, spray adhesives, hot wax, or mucilage tabs—lend a presentation a custom-made, one-of-a-kind look.

Color photographs can give vibrancy to a portfolio, and are especially important for the presentation of interior architecture; see, for example, the portfolios shown on pages 68–68 and 93–96. Though transparencies produce

Your portfolio is not simply a representation of skill and experience nor is it a pictorial annotation to your resume. Your portfolio delivers a self-portrait of you as a designer: how you think, what your sensibilities are, what your process is, how cognizant you are of the design personality you are presenting and what you are trying to tell the viewer by the pieces you have included. The making of a portfolio is a design problem with a concept, a budget, a program, as well as a final product and a mechanism through which you communicate your individual design philosophy.

Patricia Belton Oliver, AIA, Chair
Department of Environmental Design
Art Center College of Design

sharper images than inexpensive color prints, they require special handling. As a rule of thumb, the larger the color film used, the better the reproduction. As a practical matter, however, the cameras necessary to use 8″ x 10″ film and the cost of processing it put these transparencies beyond the budget of the student designer. Even 4″ x 5″ transparencies may not be feasible. More common and accessible to students are 35mm slides. These are harder to view, since reviewers may not have projection equipment available or want to take the time to set it up.

Transparencies are delicate and must be protected in some manner. Mount large ones under a black board with a cut-out window, with a sheet of clear protective acetate (mylar) over the slide. A sheet of translucent acetate placed behind the slide will diffuse any sharp lighting when the slide is held up for viewing.

Protect 35mm slides by inserting them in vinyl sleeves and be sure each slide is labeled and captioned. If you are taking them to an interview, don't expect the interviewer to provide projection equipment; bring along a loupe (a small magnifying lens that can be used to view slides against a light), a viewer, or a portable light box. Clean the dust from slides before you include them, and keep them clean (a can of compressed air and a soft brush, available from photographic supply stores, are useful for this purpose).

With the growing accessibility of comput-

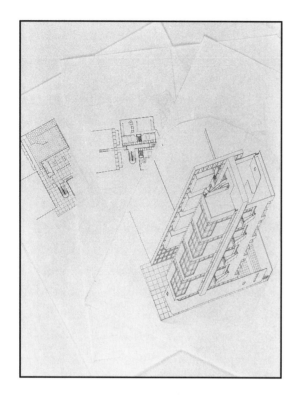

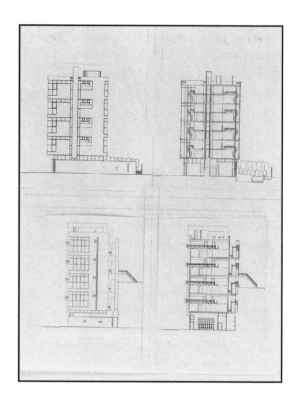

Varied materials, from conceptual sketches and bubble diagrams to finished renderings, perspectives, models, and built structures, are appropriate for inclusion in the portfolio.
Alex Pugliese, New York Institute of Technology, New York NY.
8 1/2" x 11"

Kofi Boone, The University of Michigan, Ann Arbor MI. 17" x 11"

ers and sophisticated software in the studio and at home, many more options are becoming available for the alteration of photographic images. However, the more you discover about how to manipulate images on the computer, the more you must keep in mind your final goal—to produce a high-quality, flat graphic image that works on the page. Follow the same principles of clarity and simplicity in designing computer images that you would follow without the computer. You may find that the computer is primarily valuable to you not in terms of original design, but to correct defects in photographic work. Poorly lighted areas can be digitally retouched, and color balance can be changed for greater contrast.

Composing page designs with more than one form of visual material—models, sketches, plans and other projections—can often assist the reviewer in understanding the project. For example, in Andrew Tinucci's portfolio (page 54) light has been manipulated so that the shadows emphasize the geometry of the models' structure. The professional portfolio of Professor John Reese (pages 50–51) shows, among other things, fine examples of how to present clear photographs and graphic reproductions. The design focuses attention on the illustrations by the use of a spacious layout and restrained typography. Ian Scott Sheard's portfolio (page 57) combines photographs and photostats with strong visual impact.

Kofi Boone, The University of Michigan, Ann Arbor MI. 17″ x 11″

Assuming that you have a body of work to

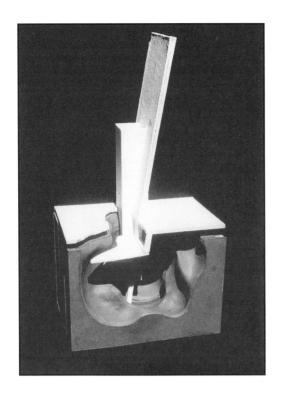

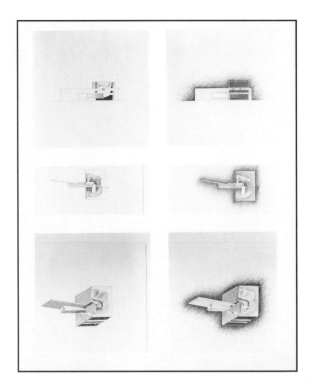

Piotr Redlinski, Pratt Institute, Brooklyn NY.
8" x 10"

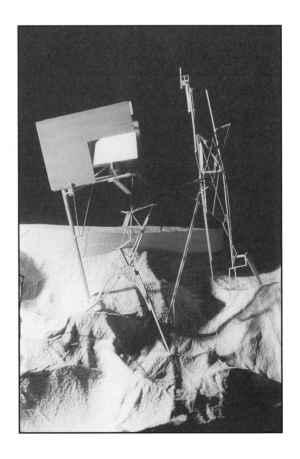

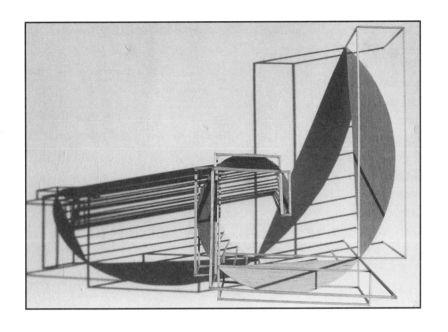

Design professionals, for the most part, rely on graphic images to communicate, record, and test ideas as well as solve problems. Through a wide range of visual media, I am able to quickly communicate and explore design images that are more expressive than words alone can convey. A well-organized, representative body of work that reveals a diverse range of abilities demonstrates the depth of involvement of the designer. In this sense, a portfolio is an essential record of growth, as well as a vehicle of communication.

William Allen, Professor
Department of Architecture and Landscape
   Design
College of Architecture and Design
Lawrence Technological University

draw upon, the portfolio design process begins with an analysis of your objectives. Is this portfolio to be part of an application for advanced education, or employment, or for participation in an actual design project as part of a competition or a grant program? In general, a portfolio to be used as part of an application for admission to graduate school should show the broadest number of varied interests and aptitudes. For an employment application, this is probably an equally valid approach, though many architectural and design firms specialize in a particular kind of work, and your knowledge of what the reviewers are looking for may help you to focus the selection of work more narrowly. Nevertheless, if you are looking for a job, a varied group of projects will convey the breadth of work that you can handle.

If you have been out of school for several years, it may not be wise to include school projects in a portfolio accompanying an application for employment unless the pieces are exceptional or especially relevant. Reviewers will want to see what you have been doing since you received your degree or became licensed. For a general portfolio, you should gradually replace school work with professional projects as they accumulate. It is appropriate to include a really fine undergraduate or graduate project, but make sure it is clear that you have been active since leaving school. (Bear in mind that the need to keep your portfolio up to date requires the choice of a flexible format and consistent methods of photographing or re-

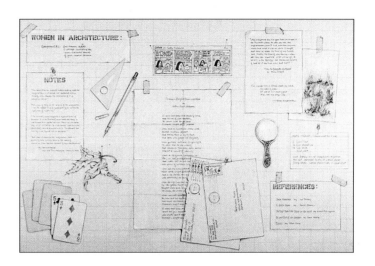

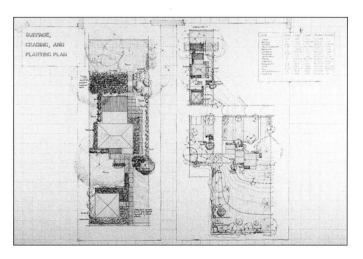

These design presentation boards present a collage of architectural elements in a soft and intriguing illusory space. These plates also exemplify graphic consistency of theme: the grid serves as a unifying element across the three plates.

Gretchen Rudy
Lawrence Technological University
Southfield, MI

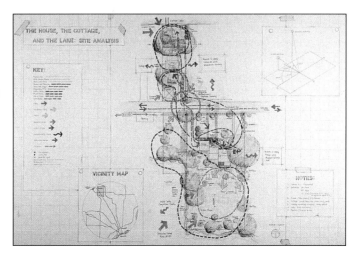

Interior and environmental design work for a senior thesis, "North Coast Harbor: Pier Park Development Concept," was presented in the form of a slide portfolio, a common practice among artists and designers.

The selections shown here demonstrate the student's high-caliber rendering skills. From top to bottom, the retired steamship USS *William G. Matthew*, docked for dining at North Coast Harbor Pier Park; café *al fresco* aboard the transformed ship; and Pier Park overlooking Lake Erie; an aerial view of Pier Park, with North Coast Harbor and the Cleveland skyline visible in the distance; the seam of land and lake at Pier Park; and a model of Pier Park structures (1/8"=1'0").

Corbin Pulliam
Cleveland Institute of Art
Cleveland, OH

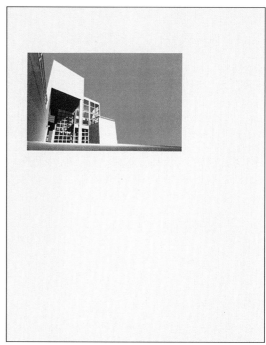

In this portfolio, a typographic first page of text is followed by a dramatic visual sequence in color. These computer-generated images begin with a small exterior view, positioned at the top of the page, and the images become successively larger or "closer" until an interior view dominates the page. The sequence demonstrates a remarkable sensitivity to the arts of animation and choreography.

Clive Lonstein, University of Miami, Miami FL

producing your work. If you begin with a small-sized looseleaf binding system and later find that a project intended for the portfolio is best represented on large-sized unbound sheets, you will be faced with assembling a whole new portfolio.)

In a portfolio designed to win a grant or competition, the focus will be narrow; you may be designing the entire portfolio around the solution to one architectural or design problem, or you may need to demonstrate your interest in and ideas about a single theme or issue. But even in this case, demonstrating a variety of design skills may be useful. Analyzing your portfolio objectives is important because you are preparing work to be judged by other people.

Once you have established your objectives, begin a portfolio audit. This is the process by which you select and, in preliminary fashion, arrange the work that you consider relevant to include. The form on page 70 (top) is one that my students use to get into the habit of making a thorough outline. Without preliminary notes of some kind, the coordination of all the details may seem an overwhelming task. On the "storyboard" form, page 70 (bottom), students indicate in words and rough sketches an approximate sequence of projects and specific images.

The average portfolio contains at least twenty to forty pages (depending on whether you use single- or double-sided pages) that cover three to five separate projects—rarely fewer, but some portfolios may justifiably be more extensive. Too many samples reveal to

Two forms used in my portfolio classes to assist students in planning their portfolios. Preparing a thorough outline and storyboard of the work to be included is essential to avoid problems during the actual layout of the pages.

Generic shopping list of portfolio contents to be organized:
The following list should be altered , if necessary, to fit your specific content requirements.

Title Page

Opening Statement

Contents Page

Index

Art/Arch/Design Studio Coursework

Construction Documents

Computer-Aided Design & Drawing

Professional and/or Employment projects

Elective coursework

Your Work (School & Professional work)
In the space that follows, create a list of all items to be included in your portfolio. List these items in the specific sequence that they should appear in your portfolio. Once ordered, note your three strongest projects with an asterisk.

A portfolio audit form, with a reminder of the possible elements for a portfolio.

Portfolio Storyboard
Use the blocks below as pages of your portfolio. Label each page according to the sequenced list of contents you completed. Number the pages accordingly.

A portfolio storyboard.

reviewers an inability to be selective, as well as a lack of respect for their time; they may simply pass by an oversize portfolio without looking at it. In addition, carrying or shipping a portfolio that has become too heavy or bulky is a problem for you.

During the portfolio audit, lay out your work in piles on a table or floor, or place it in folders. Discard the weaker projects. Arrange what you have chosen in order of importance, and sort and select the pieces within each project.

Think of the organization of your portfolio as building a bridge. Choose your very best work as the main supports. A strong piece of work should open the portfolio; another should support the middle of the presentation, and yet another should close the portfolio. The final impression is almost as important as the first impression; moreover, viewers often scan a portfolio from back to front, making the final piece of work the first that they see. The remaining work serves as the intermediate supports of your structure.

If you have enough work, an especially effective arrangement is to begin with two or three strong projects and end with a one of equal weight, with the less important pieces in between. Sequencing is a complex issue we will take up in the next chapter, but during the audit you want to make certain that you devote the most space to your best work. If you have a strong project that was poorly executed (weak photography, sketching, or site plan, for example), redo it. Sometimes this is a difficult decision to make; as you grow more experienced, you will find that what once seemed like a strong project has lost its appeal, but that is part of the process of learning. And it is why your portfolio should be designed to be frequently updated and reassembled.

The advice to place strong projects in a particular location within a portfolio is not a license to put weak or poorly executed projects between them. Set aside weak projects. There should be nothing in the portfolio that you have to apologize for or explain, nothing that will cause the reviewer to wonder why it is there at all. You are choosing among your good projects and your best projects, and the harder that decision is to make, the more you can be sure you are on the right track. Nothing in your portfolio should be simply filler. Such inclusions are embarrassing and counterproductive. Professionals who review portfolios frequently say that one of the most common failings of graduates is to include too much work that is only average in quality.

Most portfolios are project oriented, but you can also add additional samples of particular kinds of work at the end if you want to show an area of special strength, such as sketches, watercolors, photography, models.

Over-all, choose a variety of samples, from preliminary sketches to finished renderings to models, to represent each project (see, for example, the portfoios of Kofi Boone, pages 60–61, and Piotr Redlinski, pages 62–63). As noted earlier, reviewers appreciate the inclusion of conceptual drawings to show how your thinking has evolved. They are interested as

Beginning a portfolio requires you to take a step back from the reality of your own design work and to be an unemotional observer. Learning to be observant about the strengths and weaknesses of one's work in school encourages the development of a critical and unbiased eye useful to the portfolio design process and a professional career.

Betty-Lee Seydler-Sweatt
Assistant Dean
Lawrence Technological University

much in concept development as in the finished project.

As you are auditing your work, make preliminary notes about how to show each piece of work or each group of images. Whether on a simple list, a spreadsheet, or a storyboard, include the title of the project and list its component pieces, with planned sizes for the page or double-page spread. Note whether the items are drawings or photographs, and whether any special treatment, such as a fold-out, is necessary. Note the appropriate reproduction method.

Include in the audit procedure what text materials are to be included: title page, table of contents, design statement, captions, index. A resume is appropriate if the portfolio is a general presentation of your work for further schooling or employment. A listing of course work, your employment history, and list of projects completed are possible inclusions.

Once you have selected a body of work, you can estimate the overall size of the portfolio, the number of pages or plates necessary, as well as consider what format and materials will work best and what type of enclosing system or binder is appropriate.

Many students explore a wide range of paper products in their search for innovative materials. Textured papers may be appropriate for original art. For mounting art, some use soft-colored papers in neutral gray and soft earth tones, and this may be a good approach for your work, but keep in mind that mounting graphics and text on colored or tinted paper can actually distract from the images and make the text harder to read. The most frequent choice is still white paper or board. Specialty materials such as translucent bond, translucent printing paper, translucent bristol, and transparent card stock are increasingly popular, because they offer a way to separate text from background visuals.

When you have made your choices about these issues, you can make a reasonable estimate of the art materials you will need— matte boards, acetate sheets, transfer type—and their cost. Plan to make at least one duplicate portfolio, for yourself; more copies if you are making multiple submissions. Extra prints of photographs and a supply of extra art materials are useful to have on hand, since the portfolio may suffer some damage as it makes the rounds. (This may not be necessary for practice or "rehearsal" portfolios you prepare while learning to design them, but it is essential planning for the real world.)

Thumbnail layout sheets (opposite) give you the opportunity to sketch out the relative size and position of the work you have selected in more detail than the storyboard. Careful thumbnailing prevents mistakes that could force you to abandon work at midpoint and start over from scratch.

Decisions about sizing art or photographs and the treatment of them depend upon the amount of detail they contain and their dramatic impact on the page. Reverse images—

Sample thumbnail sketches, one for a horizontal format, the other for a vertical format, showing some possible layouts.

that is, white on black background—can be very effective for architectural plans, but at large sizes negative images can be overwhelming, and white type reproduced against a black background can be difficult to read. Photostats provide high contrast between black and white areas but reproduce areas of gray tone or shading poorly or not at all. You must match the reproduction technique to the artwork and decide what will work best for each image.

The portfolio audit is complete when you have assembled all the work to be included in the portfolio and have developed an idea of the order of projects within the presentation and the relative "weight" or emphasis that each project should receive. The more exact this is, the better, though it is common for problems and surprises to arise during the final assembly. Keep your audit notes at hand during all stages of the procedure. Like any other complex project, the more complete the plan, the easier the execution. The more thought you put into the audit process, the more likely it is that the portfolio will proceed quickly and without problems.

The next step is to fit the selected projects into a general format and choose the page size and enclosing system. The first decision is between vertical and horizontal formats; a less common alternative is a square format. Review your material and consider which orientation will give you the greatest freedom of design. Some materials demand a large, sweeping horizontal format to capture their scope; others require a large format of either

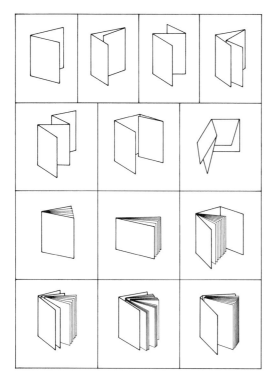

Seven methods of page folding: bifold, trifold (inward), trifold (zigzag), parallel, accordion, gate fold, cross fold; and six traditional bookbinding methods.

orientation to permit the discovery of fine detail. Smaller formats offer handling convenience and perhaps greater intimacy, but require tighter organization. Students often use two facing vertical pages of medium size to create a large horizontal format, say 40" by 60", by planning the design to run across the gutter. What is gained here is the convenience of carrying and storing the portfolio in the smaller format, and expanding it for presentation. Never choose a format based on the idea that you can lay out some pages vertically and others horizontally, so that the viewer is forced to constantly twirl the portfolio around to read it.

The actual page size is determined in part by your design decisions and in part by your technical and financial resources. Will your pages or plates and your enclosing system be unusual and handcrafted, will you trim pages yourself to a nonstandard size; or will you depend upon standard, commercially available materials? Standard page sizes, available through most paper wholesalers, print shops, and photocopy centers, are 8 1/2" x 11", 11" x 14", and 11" x 17". Looking at your work, consider whether one of these will allow the viewer to see the details as well as the full image. Review your portfolio audit and note the largest sizes of the visual materials that you have planned to include. This will generally point you toward the correct page size, though if one or two images must be sized significantly larger than the others, you might consider folding them down in a "gatefold" to fit in a portfolio de-

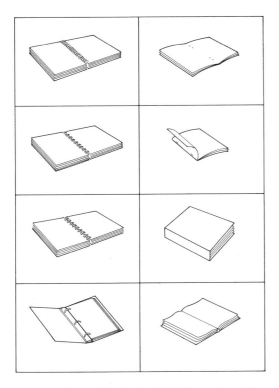

Eight traditional methods of binding: wire coil, sewn, double coil, side-stitched (stapled), comb, hinged folder, three-ring, adhesive (perfect) bound.

signed for the average image size. It is simply a problem of determining what is the size of the largest element you wish to place in a container. If the largest piece fits, all the others will fit. Generally speaking, larger page sizes permit greater flexibility in placing individual elements and in creating effective photocollages, groups of smaller images laid over larger ones.

The color, weight, and texture of the background is important as well. A neutral color—white, black, and gray tones—usually works best. Earth tones and pastels can be used if the circumstances are right; strong colors may detract from the impact of the images or create irritating contrasts. Whether you choose smooth or textured stock, paper or board, and other paper characteristics will depend on the content and format of your portfolio.

Format—the physical definition of your portfolio—includes the method of page construction and binding system. Most portfolios use one of the traditional book-binding systems (opposite); loose plates are less usual because of the packaging and sequencing problems they present.

Once you have determined the size of the pages or plates and format, it is time to choose an enclosing system. The enclosing system must be coordinated with the graphic design of the pages, as indeed it must also be related to format and binding. Although for purposes of discussion we deal with these items individually, all of them are interrelated and must be adjusted as the overall design develops.

The first question to ask yourself is whether the pages fit into commercially available binders. Commercially manufactured portfolio cases come in a number of standard sizes designed to conform to standard paper sizes. They are convenient, widely accepted among those who review portfolios, and certainly no more expensive than the art materials required to handcraft your own container. For this reason, most students and young professionals choose the common 8 1/2" x 11" page size, for which there are many binders available. One frequently used strategy is to prepare reproductions of highly detailed drawings, such as construction documents, in the larger 11" x 14" or 11" x 17" format and then double- or triple-fold them into the standard 8 1/2" x 11" acetate inserts that fit the commercial binders. Most commercially manufactured cases are sold with these acetate sheets, and you can purchase them from several manufacturers. You can cut open these acetate inserts to customize the insertion of 11" x 14" vertical sheets or 11" x 14" horizontal sheets.

Another simple solution is to use a commercial sketchbook, as illustrated in the example at left.

Though you may not want to include original drawings if your portfolio is going to circulate out of your hands, reviewers like to see original art. If you use originals, you should protect them by placing them in acetate sleeves, or between dye-cut boards, or simply by slipping a piece of translucent paper between the sheets of drawing paper.

Simple artist's sketchbook
used as portfolio by the author.

Sleeves do add a reflective barrier that makes viewing of the artwork more difficult, and acetate tears easily. Stronger plastic protective sleeves are available, but translucent rather than transparent ones, fine for holding slides, are unsuitable since they obscure the art.

Most portfolios are either 8 1/2" x 11" or the size of another commercial binder, or custom-bound in a box or a hand-made binder. A large or nonstandard page size will almost certainly compel you to use a binder, box, or container that you construct yourself, but there are other good reasons to choose unconventional page sizes and noncommercial binders. You can size images with much greater freedom, and the work will look less confined. Nonstandard or oversize pages stand out. However, if your portfolio is oversize, be sure that the pages are securely attached or that the binding is adequate to support them. Pages that fall to the floor are soon damaged. And in choosing an unusual formats, be reasonable. If you can't comfortably carry and view your portfolio, neither will anyone else.

A number of nonstandard and hand-crafted enclosing systems are shown on pages 80–81. A loose-leaf-style binder is shown, as well as some elegant methods of enclosing unbound plates. Brad Burkhardt, an environmental design student, put his portfolio in a hand-made aluminum case. Phyllis Semenuik used two broad elastic bands attached together asymmetrically to hold her unbound plates, while Natalia

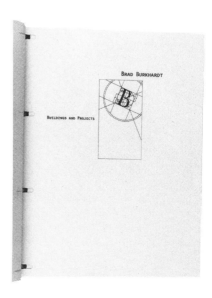

A handmade aluminum binder.
Brad Burkhardt, Parsons School of Design,
New York NY. 10″ x 14″

A mini-portfolio, this consists of small
plates enclosed between boards held
together by broad elastic bands.
Phyllis Semenuik, Technical University
of Nova Scotia, Halifax, Nova Scotia.
5″ x 7″

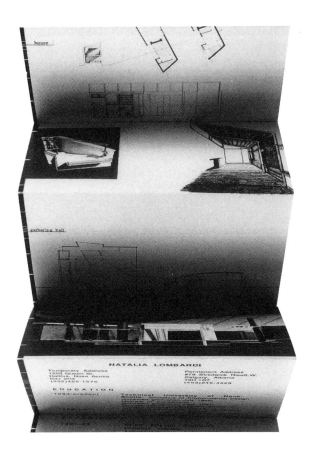

Another attractive mini-portfolio, by a faculty member at the Technical University of Nova Scotia, is wrapped like a gift with decorative paper strips and folds out into a stand-up presentation. Natalia Lombardi, Technical University of Nova Scotia, Halifax, Nova Scotia. 4 1/2" x 5 3/4"

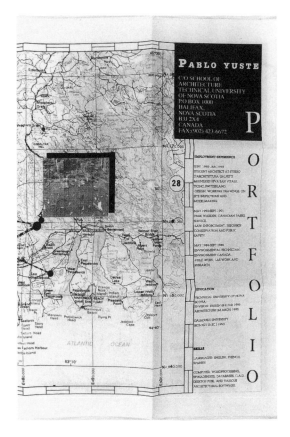

This mini-portfolio is designed like a road map. Pablo Yuste, Technical University of Nova Scotia, Halifax, Nova Scotia. 5 1/2" square (folded), 17" x 22" (open)

Lombardi's portfolio unfolds horizontally as a kind of continuous scroll held between boards with a decorative ribbon. A mini-portfolio, it measures 4 1/4" x 5 3/4" when folded. Pablo Yuste's portfolio unfolds in both directions like a map. Yuste's work is also a mini-portfolio, measuring 5 1/2" square when closed and 17" x 22" when opened. Another fold-out arrangement, bound between boards in the traditional book form, is shown on page 93.

In choosing an enclosing system, look for simple, stable, and sturdy construction. A binder that falls apart in the hands of the reviewer or is difficult to handle makes a poor impression. Your portfolio will be passed around among many people and may not always be treated gently. It must be designed to endure use, and you must maintain it. A defective mechanism in the binder will irritate those who must open it, and denotes a lack of professionalism. Spiral or permanent binders are more suitable for a "dedicated" project that is unlikely to need updating. With bound pages, both sides of the paper are generally used. Unbound plates or ring binders make it easy to rearrange or add new projects over the years. With unbound plates, you will probably reproduce images only on one side of the page, and this may be costly in terms of available space. Unbound plates may also get out of order: if you choose this style, be sure that they are clearly numbered.

In terms of style, the enclosing system should be visually appealing but understated in a simple and tasteful way. It should reveal

Limited resources should not be a deterrent to putting forth the maximum effort when designing a portfolio. The use of basic materials in a well-designed product indicates many things—among them creativity and thoughtfulness.

Kathryn T. Prigmore, AIA
Associate Dean
School of Architecture and Planning
Howard University

both a sense of imagination and serious professionalism. The materials, the color, the finish, the detailing should be striking, but not garish. The package should not be more exciting than its contents. Most commercial binders are businesslike in design. Hand-made enclosing systems provide the greatest opportunity for creative experiment, and the greatest opportunity for error. Pay particular attention to the sturdiness of the design and the materials if you are crafting your own case.

The enclosing system you choose also has a bearing on the sequencing of material. The double-page spreads of a binder force you to consider exactly how long each section of the portfolio will be and how each piece of work will lay out. If one project ends on a verso (left-hand) page, what is the effect on the spread of starting a dramatically different project on the recto (right-hand) page? The number of pages devoted to each section may have to be modified to take facing-page design into account. Clearly, unbound pages avoid this problem and offer you more flexibility in arranging work, but with this arrangement you lose the option of expanding or enlarging particular elements to run across two pages. It should be obvious that you cannot prepare a portfolio in a completely linear fashion, dealing with only one design element or one decision at a time. You must learn to think not only in terms of what to include, but also in terms of how everything will fit and how consecutive pieces of work will flow into each other.

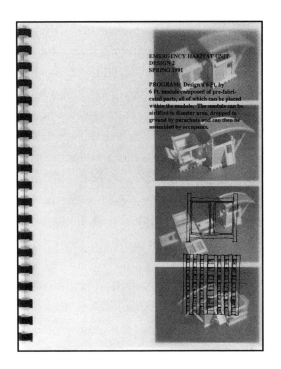

EMERGENCY HABITAT UNIT
DESIGN 2
SPRING 1991

PROGRAM: Design a 6 Ft. by
6 Ft. module composed of pre-fabri-
cated parts, all of which can be placed
within the module. The module can be
airlifted to disaster area, dropped to
ground by parachute and can then be
assembled by occupants.

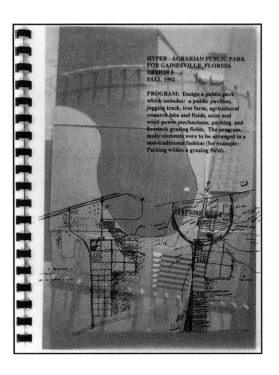

HYPER - AGRARIAN PUBLIC PARK
FOR GAINESVILLE, FLORIDA
DESIGN 5
FALL 1992

PROGRAM: Design a public park
which includes: a public pavilion,
jogging track, tree farm, agricultural
research labs and fields, solar and
wind-power mechanisms, parking, and
livestock grazing fields. The program-
matic elements were to be arranged in a
non-traditional fashion (for example:
Parking within a grazing field).

Translucent pages offer the opportunity to overlay
conceptual sketches and text on developed models.
Joseph W. Tisdale, University of Florida, Gainesville
FL. 8 1/2″ x 11″

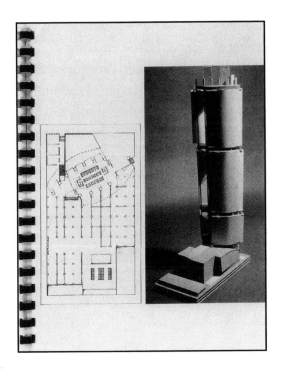

3.
Developing
the Layout

Once you have decided upon portfolio content, general format, page size, and enclosing system, you now come to the vital matter of developing the layout—that is, designing the pages, sizing the images and placing them on the pages, designing the typography for the accompanying text, and creating the text elements such as the title page, contents, design statements, and resume, and fine-tuning the sequencing or arrangement of pages within and between projects.

Begin by designing a grid, or underlying structure. The grid helps you to size and position the images in a coherent design. It is really a set of assumptions about the permissible sizes and shapes of images and blocks of text and it helps

Eight ways of aranging columns of text
on horizontal and vertical formats.

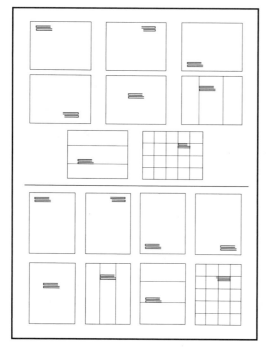

Eight ways of arranging heads
on horizontal and vertical formats.

you achieve some design consistency throughout the portfolio. It is customary to decide upon a standard "measure" or width for the material. Text and images may run across the entire width of the page, or the page may be divided into two, three, or more columns. The grid should take into consideration the character of the images: some demand large-scale reproduction; others can be reproduced small. For example, you may want to group images in sequence, showing the evolution of a concept. Break down the pages into imaginary blocks of space of stylistically related appearance, and fit images and text into these blocks. Now you can determine the final size and position of the artwork. Using the thumbnail layouts you prepared during formatting, analyze the different images and text blocks for each project and each page and position them on the grid. You may need to make a series of sketches, first perhaps in the form of roughs on smaller-size sheets, working up to a full-size "dummy" on tracing paper. This is a process of trial and error and constant adjustment to solve conceptual problems that reveal themselves as you lay out the pages. Remember that the grid of a well-organized page should be essentially invisible: it should be a guide, not a straitjacket.

It is during this development that the difficult-to-define qualities of style and vision evolve. For an important portfolio, you may want to experiment with as many as six different rehearsal studies of this kind. Working with full-scale tracing paper allows you to test

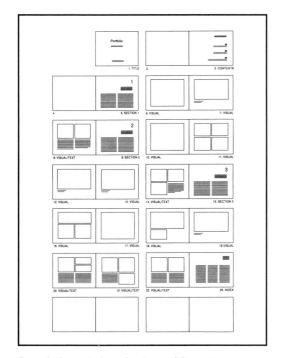

Sample layouts for a horizontal format
with headings, text, and visuals.

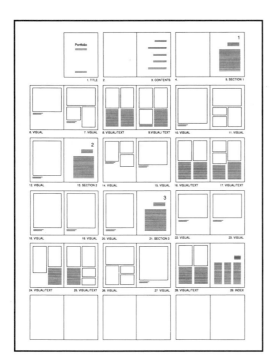

Sample layouts for a vertical format
with headings, text, and visuals.

the proposed size of each image against the page and see the effects of juxtaposition and sequence.

You can resize images easily with a proportional scale (available at most art-supply stores). The scale tells you, if images are being enlarged or reduced to a certain height, just what the width of that image will be in the new size, or if a particular width is desired, just what the new height of the image will be. Even easier, draw a diagonal line from one corner of the image to the opposite corner (on an overlay or photocopy: don't draw on original art or a photograph!), or extend the diagonal line beyond the border of the image. Any point on this line will produce a different-sized image that remains proportional to the original image (see overleaf).

As you develop the page layout from sketch to actuality, you make more detailed decisions about the size and style of text type, heads, captions, tabular materials, charts, and folios (page or plate numbers). Seldom are all these elements necessary: choose what you need to make your points. Is a project based on a class assignment or other coursework? Is a design statement helpful? Do captions repeat what is obvious in the illustrations, or offer additional information? Are relationships between visuals clear? Do details need explanation? If your portfolio consists of unbound plates, are they numbered? And don't forget that you must clearly label your portfolio, inside and out, with your name, address, and telephone number. It is counterproductive, to say the least, to submit a portfolio for review if the reviewers

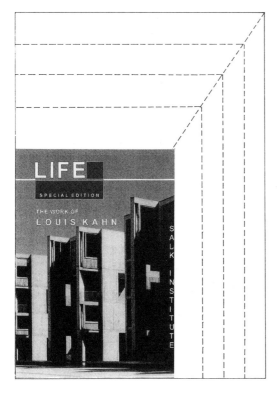

Simple method of enlarging
or reducing artwork.

have no way of contacting you or returning your presentation!

There are many options for the placement of text elements. Legibility is a prime concern; text should work with the graphic images and not compete with or obscure them. Keep the text clearly separate from the images, or maintain strong contrast between their values in order to preserve legibility of both. Serif typefaces are elegant; sans-serif typefaces tend to be functional and businesslike. Highly styled typefaces may be appropriate for heads, but generally make for poor readability. While there are thousands of typefaces available, most of them suitable for heads under some circumstances, perhaps only a dozen families of type are really suitable for extended blocks of text. Study the typefaces used in books and magazine articles, and you will see the same faces again and again. A flamboyant or overly styled face irritates and tires the eye very quickly in long blocks. Does the type and headline style that works well for one project work equally well for all the projects? Is the design consistent? Refine the presentation.

Five varied portfolios demonstrate consistent designs in with different types of images fitted into a grid structure. Arthur Hanlon's student portfolio has a horizontal format and a formal two-column vertical structure (opposite). The vertical column on the left side of the page is narrower than the column on the right side of the page. But even with this highly structured approach, there is a sense of

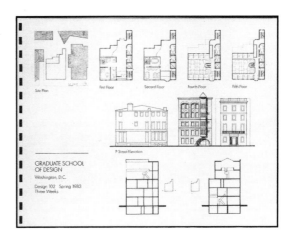

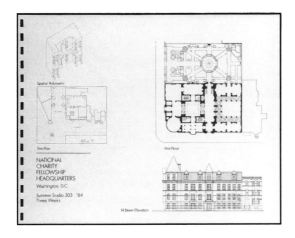

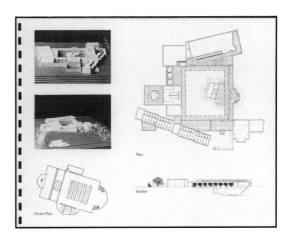

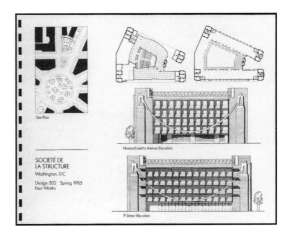

A simple but carefully constructed two-column layout.
Arthur C. Hanlon, The Catholic University of America,
Washington DC. 11″ x 8 1/2″

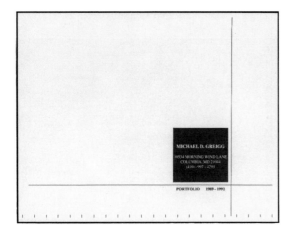

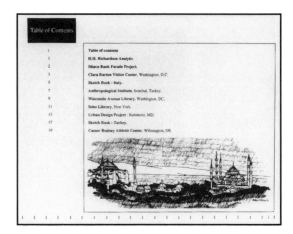

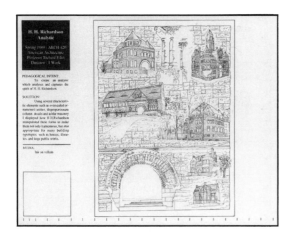

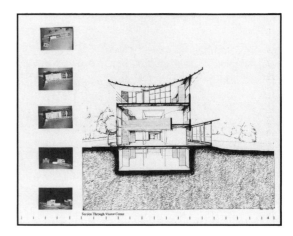

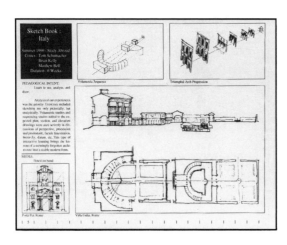

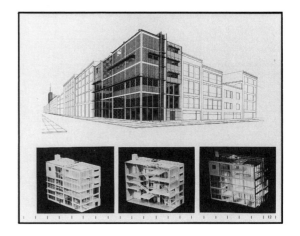

A flexible three-column grid.

Michael D. Greigg, University of Maryland, Columbia MD. 11" x 8 1/2"

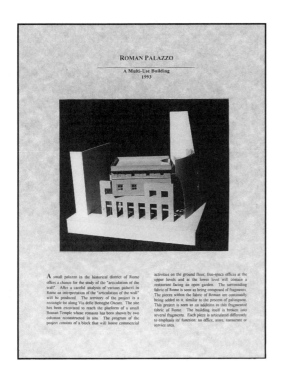

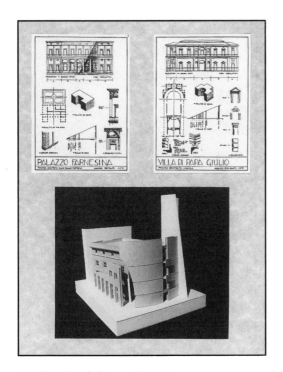

Another simple layout strategy.
Peter R. Phillips, Temple University,
Philadelphia PA. 8 1/2″ x 11″

freedom in the design, created by the flexible way the images are laid out within the grid.

Michael D. Greigg's grid has three columns on a horizontal format (opposite) . The page is divided into a fairly narrow left-hand column, used largely for text material, and two right-hand columns that can function as one wider column, as desired. In this way, he gained a great deal of flexibility with the right side of the page, which is used for large images or groups of smaller ones.

The portfolio of Peter R. Phillips (left) has a vertical format and a formal two-column design for the text, with headings and images centered above the text. Placing text above and below the graphic elements on the project opening pages helps to focus attention on the graphic elements.

Carlos Brun began with a transparent overlay of typographic elements that also defines the grid pattern for the smaller peripheral graphic images on subsequent pages (pages 92–93). Text and photographs are laid on top of other images at an angle to break the rigidity of the grid pattern and convey a feeling of openness and drama.

Muhammad Muzaffar used a repeated graphic element—a border—to help define the grid pattern of his horizontal pages (page 98). The device breaks the page into separate areas for text and images. Such decoration must be used cautiously to avoid unwanted distractions or disturbing contrasts of shape and form between the subject matter and the decorative elements.

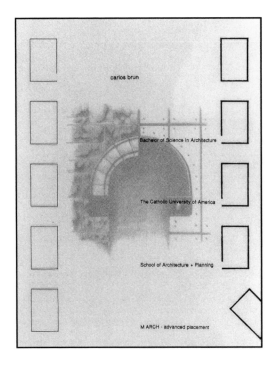

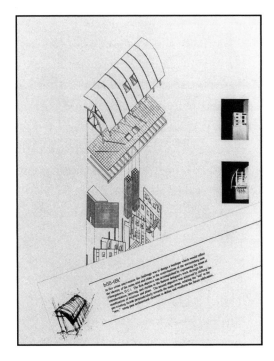

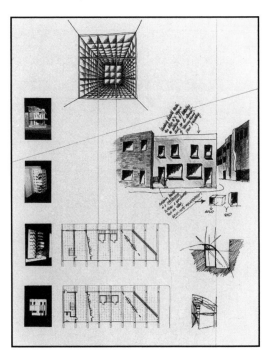

In this portfolio, submitted in application to a graduate program, the subtle grid is skillfully
interrupted with diagonals to create a memorable sequence of lively graphic statements.
Carlos Brun, University of Miami, Coral Gables FL. 8 1/2″ x 11″

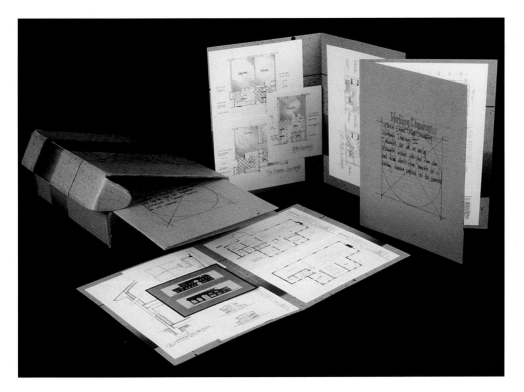

A corrugated cardboard box and 8 1/2″ x 11″ folders of speckled paper with
hand-lettered titles make simple but effective packaging for this interior design
student's application to graduate school.

Frederick Vasquez, Lawrence Technological University, Southfield MI

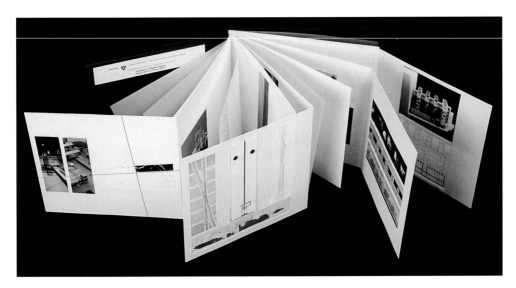

This handmade hard-back binder with bi- and tri-fold pages, sewn and glued
in place, holds a broad array of reprographic elements, including photostats,
cibachrome photographs, and other graphic arts materials.

Rachael Eberts, Parsons School of Design, New York NY

Graphics/Color Rendering

From the graduate portfolio of a landscape architecture student, this 8 1/2" x 11" page from a wire-bound portfolio shows strength in draftsmanship and sketching.

Elizabeth Saunders
Ohio State University
Columbus, OH

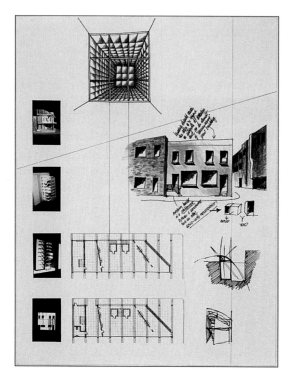

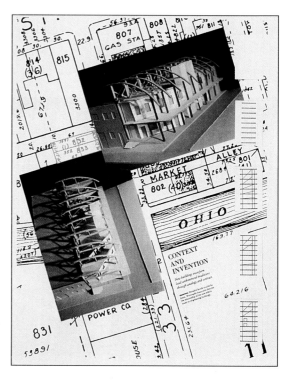

Submitted as part of a graduate program application, this portfolio conveys a dynamic vitality through the use of diagonals that interrupt its subtle underlying grid.

Carlos Brun, University of Miami, Coral Gables FL

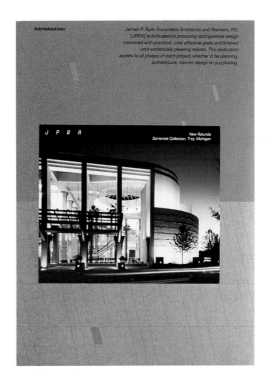

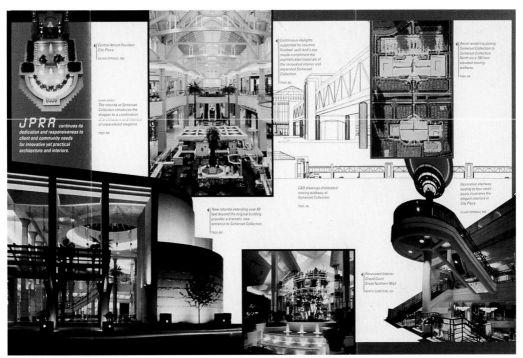

This is part of a promotion piece prepared by J. P. Ryan & Associates.
The 9″ x 12″ brochure demonstrates sophisticated use of presentation tools:
die-cuts, folding panels, inserts, and full-color printing.

J. P. Ryan & Associates, Farmington Hills MI

These pieces from a student portfolio display strong computer skills; the renderings were done with AutoCAD and three-dimensional modeling programs.

Christopher Michael Garrison, Lawrence Technological University, Southfield MI

A portfolio is an opportunity to showcase what you have done and how you did it. It also gives the reviewer a real sense of what you are capable of doing. Simple or complex, it needs to reflect how you think and who you are.

Arthur L. Kaha, AIA
School of Architecture
University of Illinois at Urbana-Champaign

Three rehearsal portfolios from my Professional Portfolio course (pages 99–101) illustrate still other layout solutions. Amy Oliver used a horizontal format, and reproduced the text in white against a black background. Matthew Coates used a vertical format with text overlays and folded panels, with identifying text placed within a black panel on the left margin. Elaine Keiser chose a horizontal format, fold-out panels, and a grid that divided the plate both vertically and horizontally into rectangular blocks, very like a book.

In Taha Al-Douri's imaginative and graphically sophisticated portfolio, the images are sensitively composed within the black foamcore rectangular mount (page 102). The use of the 35mm frame is a unifying feature. Although the shrinkwrap creates a reflective surface, it is no more reflective than acetate sleeves and does not diminish clarity and legibility. The color illustrations are enclosed in a professionally hand-crafted wooden box with a brass hinge and clasp for security during mailing.

The portfolio of James P. Ryan Associates, specialists in the design and construction of large shopping malls, was printed in four colors using special inks with a metallic finish, superimposed photographic images, with die-cut portions, tearsheet inserts, and double-folded panels (see page 95). Such ambitious promotional brochures are naturally much more costly than individual designers and students can afford.

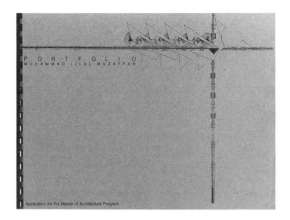

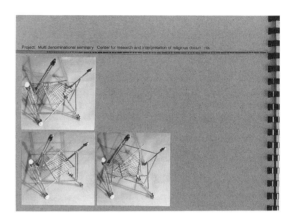

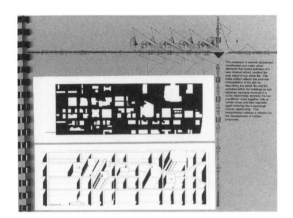

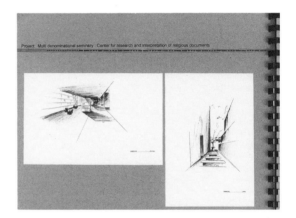

A decorative border separates text and visual elements
and produces a unifying theme in this portfolio.
Muhammad Muzaffar, Arizona State University,
Tempe AZ. 11″ x 8 1/2″

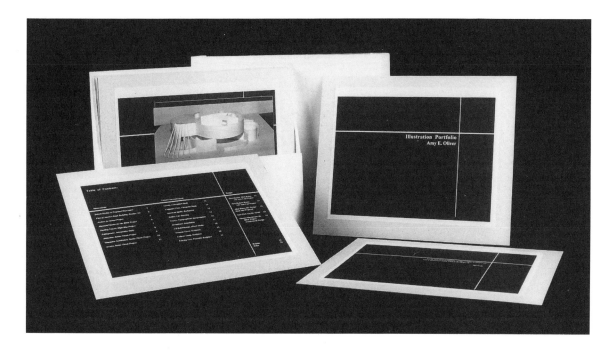

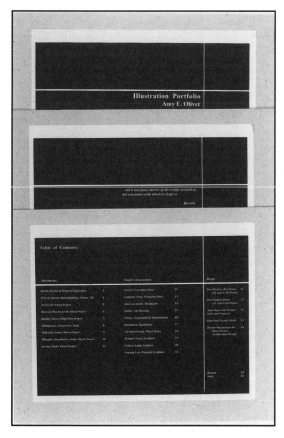

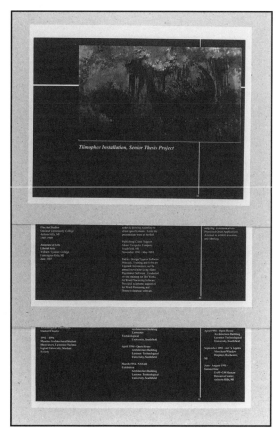

Rehearsal portfolio: unbound plates with text reversed out of a black background.

This is a highly graphic treatment.

Amy Oliver, Lawrence Technological University, Southfield MI. 11″ x 8 1/2″

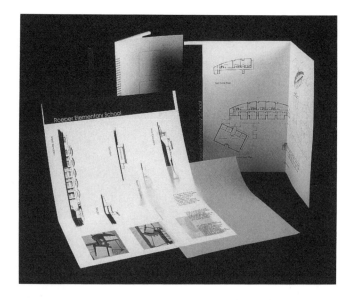

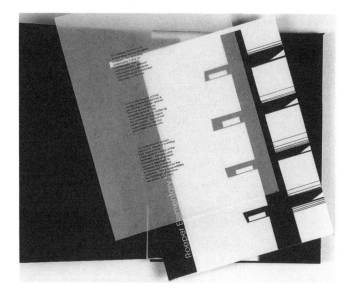

Rehearsal portfolio: unbound plates with double- and multiple-folding pages. Each plate is contained in a black, hand-crafted cardboard sleeve.
Matthew Coates,
Lawrence Technological University,
Southfield MI. 9″ x 12″

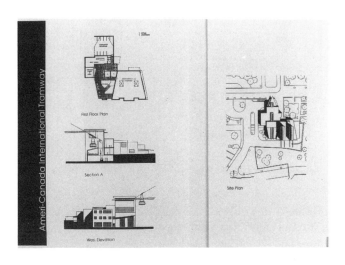

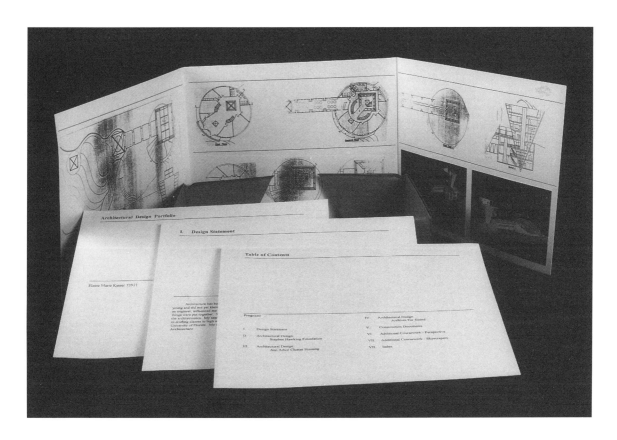

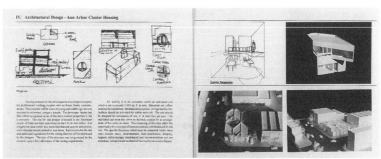

Rehearsal portfolio: unbound plates with double
and triple fold-out pages and a strong horizontal grid.
Elaine Keiser, Lawrence Technological
University, Southfield MI. 11″ x 8 1/2″

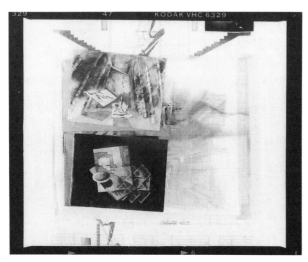

This portfolio of architectural illustrations uses the device
of a 35mm-film frame as the unifying structure.
Taha A. Al-Douri, Pennsylvania State University,
University Park PA. 11″ x 8 1/2″

The final problem of portfolio design is achieving the best possible sequence of images for the most effective impact on the reviewer. Preliminary decisions about the ordering of material are made during the portfolio audit, but it is during the actual layout, while you are sizing and placing graphics on the page, that you discover how effectively the original plan will work, and make adjustments accordingly.

Two levels of sequencing need to be considered: the order and manner in which projects are presented and the transitions between different projects and the sequence of images within each project.

You may simply string projects one after the other, but one of the most common errors in portfolio design is failure to make it clear where one project leaves off and another begins. The confusion occurs especially when different media—photographs, photostats, drawings, site plans—are used. Consider developing a standard divider page, like the chapter opening in a book, or some other visual signal of change, like a strong, well-designed heading. Another aid to the viewer is a "running" head identifying the project at the top or bottom of each page. You may know the content of your own work so well that the transitions seem clear. But without effective signposts, what is obviously a new project to you may seem like a new view of the previous project to someone not familiar with your work.

The number and arrangement of images on a page and on a series of pages controls

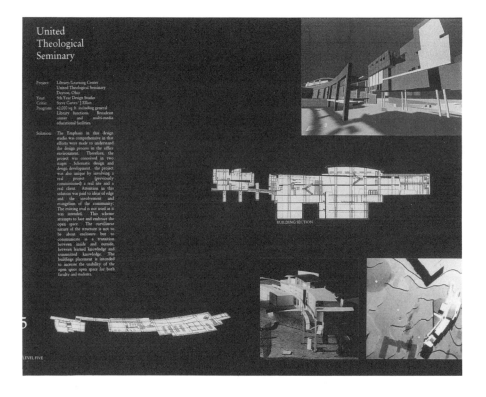

The plans lead
visually to the pho-
tographs in these
pages from a gradu-
ate portfolio.
David Powell,
Miami University,
Oxford OH.
11″ x 8 1/2″

the pace at which the reviewer is introduced to a visual problem and its solution. At the simplest level, you must always be conscious of where the reviewer's eye is being led, whether the reviewer's understanding of the your ideas is being helped or hindered, and whether the flow of ideas across the page prepares the reviewer for the next spread. And all this must be achieved while maintaining an overall consistent design for the entire presentation. Remember that in a bound portfolio the viewer's eye falls first on the right side of the right-hand page; all other things being equal, place your most important images there and use the left-hand page for secondary illustrations and text.

Sequences should have some logic or motivating force. For example, you might begin with simple pieces and work up to more complex images. Alternatively, move from exterior views of a structure to the interior, from close-ups to long views, from detail to overall, or the reverse. Start with a simple black-and-white sketch that lays out the problem, show developmental drawings, and end with the solution, rendered in a wider variety of graphic media. Search for a narrative principle conveyed in graphic terms, so the pages build on each other psychologically in the viewer's mind. To test your choices, try flipping quickly through the roughs, ignoring details and focusing on the progression of images, much as you would riffle through the pages of a cartoon flip book.

Building positive impressions quickly is your goal. You have to compress four or five

The storyboard is an invaluable tool for planning one's portfolio. It serves as the score for orchestrating the entire process. The creative designer develops many alternative strategies on the storyboard as reflections of the design process and a summary of personal design experiences. The discipline of rethinking the storyboard and the resourcefulness which an individual can bring to the planning process in its embryonic stage of development is essential. All of the attributes of a professional design education are reflected in the comprehensive organization of the portfolio, and these are extremely valuable to an individual who holds the highest ideals for future practice.

Dr. Neville Clouten, Dean
College of Architecture and Design
Lawrence Technological University

separate projects into twenty to twenty-five pages, so you have no more than five or six pages to describe each project; hence the need for choosing strong, interrelated images, without any "filler." If your portfolio is too long, the reviewer won't look at it all; even if you are presenting the portfolio in person, the reviewer may cut off your presentation. In a half-hour or hour-long interview, only about half that time will be devoted to reviewing the portfolio, and its impact must be immediate.

One of a wide variety of effective sequences is from David Powell's portfolio. The spreads on page 104 show a single project with photographs and plans, type reversed out in white against a black background. The first page uses a two-column grid with a narrow column of type, with the images stacked more or less vertically from top to bottom. On the second page the left-hand column is wider to accommodate images that lead the eye across the page.

Sequence also implies progression in the design process from preliminary conceptual studies to fully rendered illustrations and models. J. W. Tisdale's pages show early drawings overlaid on the developed model (pages 84–85).

Clive Lonstein takes a somewhat bolder approach (opposite and page 68). His introductory pages are typographic, visually appealing and easy to read. The illustrations that follow are a dramatic change of pace. A full-page self-portrait in the middle of the portfolio (not shown) signals the introduction

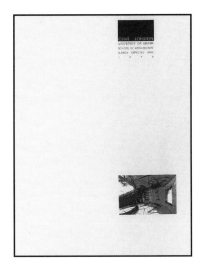

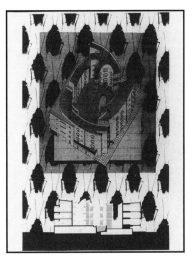

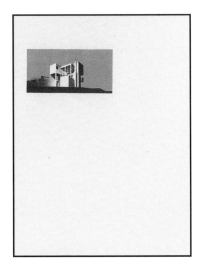
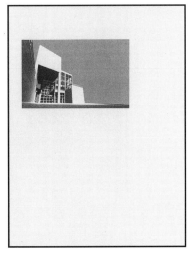

A varied and arresting sequence of text and images.
Clive Lonstein, University of Miami, Coral Gables FL. 8 1/2″ x 11″

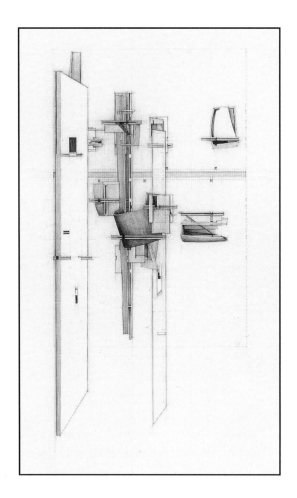

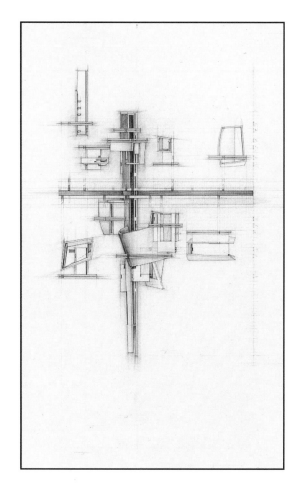

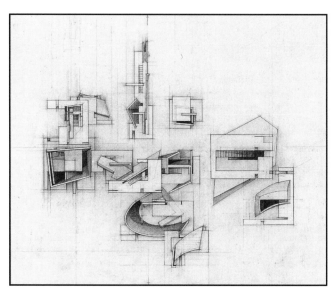

The exquisite plan and elevation views in this portfolio are ranged in "chambers" grouped in quadrants on opposite sides of an axis. The careful application of gray values and the abundant white space around the drawings give them a jewel-like character.
Thierry Landis, Pratt Institute, Brooklyn NY. 8" x 10" (top), 11 1/2" x 8" (right)

to a sequence of architectural sketches centered in white space, which reveal the designer's strong drawing skills. Another dramatic transition, with the sequence of computer-generated images that move from a small exterior view positioned at the top of the page through a progression of increasingly larger views of the interior design space, demonstrates sensitivity to the arts of animation and cinematography.

Thierry Landis's sequence of drawings (opposite), plan and elevation views of a living/working environment, was a project in twelve-tone drawing. Arranged in clustered chambers on opposite sides of an axis, with abundant white space, the drawings have a jewel-like character.

The portfolio of Tim Collett (page 110) is a good example of careful pacing. In order to separate one project from the next, Collett has grouped his projects in individual suites by delicately sewing together all the pages associated with each project, using a translucent paper cover and printed title.

John Maze's portfolio (page 111), with its regular alternation of text and graphics and varied images, presents a good solution to the problems of sequencing that confront the designer. Sequencing is as much a problem for the novelist or nonfiction writer as the designer, but the novelist can signal to the reader quite specifically in his prose when a scene is ending and what is likely to happen next. The graphic designer must accomplish the same thing with a series of visual images and a minimum of prose, and the conventions

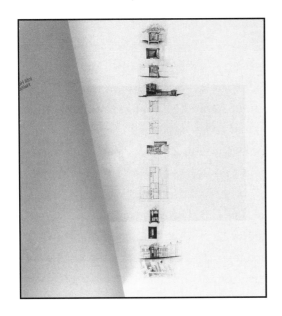

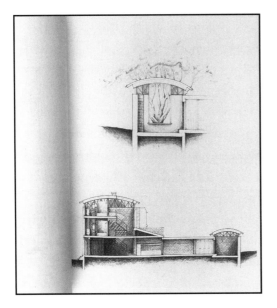

Another use of translucent overlays, in this case
to introduce the sequence of images.
Tim Collett, Technical University of Nova
Scotia, Nova Scotia. 8 1/2" x 11"

and emotional content of visual images are
more ephemeral and less clearly defined
than those of writing. Reactions to the effect
of a particular graphic design are more varied. Still, seventy years of experience with
the techniques of cinematography has taught
us quite a bit about how sequences of visual
images build their impact. Changes of scale,
focusing in on a significant detail, changes of
perspective, and varying the technique of
presentation are all part of the process. Is
there a logical and interesting flow to the
work, or does something hold you up and
stop you? It is difficult to lay out rules for sequencing because it is such an intuitive
process, but each portfolio will either have an
engaging sequence of images or it won't, and
as you gain more and more experience you
will be able to tell if you have succeeded
fairly quickly.

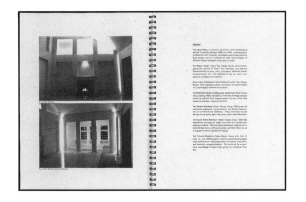

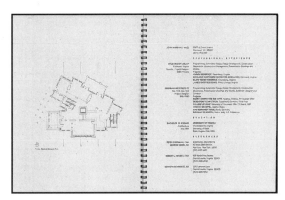

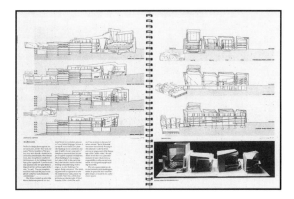

A professional's portfolio that packs a great deal of information in.
John Maze, Arizona State University, Tempe AZ. 8 1/2″ x 11″

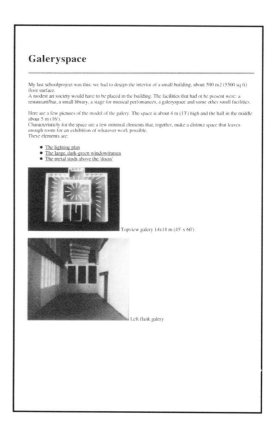

A home page and other pages on the web site of Robbert de Goede, The Netherlands.

Mirrormonument

This piece has an interesting story to it. It is my reaction on living between the scyscrapers of a big american city.
What irritated me the most about walking around between these gigantic buildings was the lack of open (quality-)space around you.
On the most beautifull days it was hardly possible to enjoy the blue sky unless you look straight up or when you stop in the middle of a big street with danger for ones own life.
Because of the mostly reflective surfaces of the buildings you don't even know what building you are actually looking at.
Since I think mother nature is still the best architect in the world this annyed me a great deal.
This piece is made to be put in the middle of a big field and will be directed on a 45 degree angle different than the street grid. This to state my disbelief on the possibility of surprise that one can encounter in a city-grid like this, to much openness is efficient for traffic, but it is also lethal for the mysticism of a city. New York is an excellent example of this. The city won't get interesting as far as everyday streetlife is concerned until you go downtown to Soho and Greenwich Village. Where the grid is not that easily regognizable.
The mirrors are 1 by 2,5 meter (±3 1/3' x 8') and between sides is 70 cm (±2 1/3') of space that one can walk through.
In the walkway are steps placed to pursue a physical experience when walking through it (6 m, 20'). This to emphasise the lack of human size in scyscrapers. Only straight up and through the slots (5 cm, 2") between the mirrors you will be able to see nature around you and can you let your eyes dwirl off.

4.
Digital Portfolios

Every design student is aware that the computer has brought about a revolution in information technology. The personal computer, in particular, combined with relatively inexpensive peripherals such as printers, scanners, modems, and CD-ROM drives, and sophisticated page-layout and illustration software, have made possible desktop publishing, which permits individuals to produce finished, high-quality graphic work from a single computer terminal or workstation. This new technology reinvents the notion of the portfolio. Not everyone has access to the necessary equipment; even today, the cost of setting up a modest desktop publishing oper-

An architectural drawing
rendered and then elongated
with Freehand™ 4.0.
Paul Matelic, Massachusetts
Institute of Technology,
Cambridge MA.

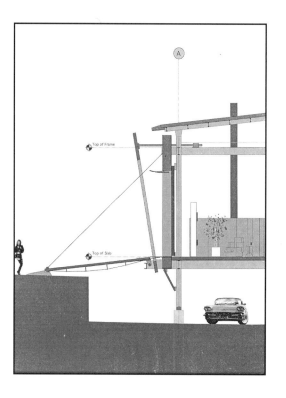

Another manipulation: a photograph was first scanned into a digital file and then altered using Photoshop™ 3.0.
Paul Matelic, Massachusetts Institute of Technology, Cambridge MA.

A ray-traced Autocad™ image brought into
Photoshop™ for additional modification, includ-
ing the addition of figures, transparency, and
lighting effects.
Paul Matelic, Massachusetts Institute of
Technology, Cambridge MA. Image by Atelier 4
International 1994.

ation is about the same as buying a used car,
not a small expense. But more and more universities and design centers are making such
equipment available, and the technology
continues to become more affordable.
Macintosh and Windows-based software,
with point and click technology, have elimi-
nated the need to learn complex computer
codes or command lines. Computers can
eliminate much of the drudgery of draftsmanship by quickly accomplishing repetitive
tasks.

The desktop revolution is not so much in
the end product, which, even on a monitor
screen presents us with a recognizable page
format, but in the freer and more varied techniques of image manipulation. Using the
computer, the size of images can be instantly
changed. Their quality can be revised or improved, making photoretouching virtually
obsolete. No longer do you need the skills of
manual paste-up, photographic reproduction,
and hand-applied typography. Paul Matelic's
work opposite and at left are examples of
architectural illustrations in which various
elements have been redesigned and
expanded through digital manipulation,
while the work of three undergraduate students (page 116) demonstrates the use of the
computer for three-dimensional modeling.
The sample from Gary Davis's portfolio
shows the dramatic contrasts that can be
achieved by manipulating light and shadow,
while the pieces by Sean McCarry and
Gabriel Siejas show more subtle gradations
of light and the use of dramatic perspective.

Three architectural illustrations made with
computer imaging systems.

Gary Davis, New Jersey Institute
of Technology, Newark NJ

Sean McCarry, New Jersey Institute
of Technology, Newark NJ

Gabriel Siejas, New Jersey Institute
of Technology, Newark NJ

Almost any image—drawings and photographs, color prints, transparencies, and film negatives—can be scanned into digital files or created from scratch electronically. Digital cameras, like those that record images for television broadcasting, will soon yield the quality of the best conventional cameras, rendering the process of photographic developing unnecessary.

Of course, digital technology is only as good as the reproduction methods that are available. But high-end digital printers are now achieving a quality of reproduction that rivals traditional photolithography. High-resolution laser printers can now almost match the quality of photographic printing processes, and less expensive inkjet printers offer reasonable test prints.

And now the Internet is revolutionizing the way information is transmitted and made available. More and more professional organizations, corporations, and individuals are establishing web sites. Many now offer a multitude of pictures and architectural plans from buildings around the world—virtual portfolios. Many universities maintain their own "servers" and offer Internet connections to their students as an integral part of program studies. If you have a computer and a modem, the Internet is certainly worth exploring. Go to one of the Web's popular indexes, such as Yahoo or the Whole Internet Catalog, and click on Architecture. You can find a great deal of career information, job listings, grant applications, and announcements of competitions, even a collection of visual images providing a mini-history of Renaissance architecture. The information available on the Internet is growing by leaps and bounds every day.

For many college students, the first introduction to web publishing (or broadcasting) of their portfolios occurs during their undergraduate years or in graduate school, when they use web sites hosted by their own university.

More and more students today are becoming "wired" and versed in HTML (Hyper Text Modeling Language) coding. They can quickly put up basic web pages and/or sites from which to broadcast. In order for Frederick Gibson of Seattle to present his web portfolio (pages 120–121) he digitized his work, or digitally created parts of it directly on the computer. His portfolio includes sample pages, architectural project designs, and even fly-throughs. He describes his web portfolio this way, "If you would like to experience the full depth of my professional portfolio in real time on the internet's world wide web (www), please jump to http://www.gibson-design.com. One of the fascinating aspects of publishing on the web is the ability to enrich and expand content with no concern for printing costs. The only limitation is time itself. I plan to have my entire portfolio, including photos, images, plans, sketches, construction photos, writings, and additional VRML (Virtual Reality Modeling Language) by the end of the summer, 1996. My current vision is to use the www as the complete archive of my past and current work with as

Oftentimes a portfolio is the only quick reference available for past design projects. Because it is a working document, it should be updated during each project. With the time pressures placed upon a professional design studio, there is never time to go back!

**Scott A. Erdy, Associate
The Hillier Group
Princeton, New Jersey**

much detail as the visitor would like to see throughout my career. An even more fascinating development on the www is the arrival of VRML. With VRML a visitor can 'virtually' walk and fly through a computer-generated 3D environment. Although not as good as an actual site visit, VRML lets anyone on the web explore the environments I design—an incredibly powerful way to experience my design portfolio."

Today, firms can look at current portfolios as well as in-progress studio work to find prospective employees. The process of computer-assisted design critique can occur anywhere, anytime, regardless of location. A student can assemble a simple home page with multiple pages and broadcast it throughout the world, as illustrated by the samples of Robbert de Goede's portfolio from the Netherlands (pages 112–114).

At the Harvard Graduate School of Design, students work with visiting professors who lecture at the university once a week and offer critical opinions and design dialogue online. The Design Studio of the Future, a graduate architectural design studio at M.I.T., took place entirely online and in communication with five affiliated international universities. Students shared a database as well as wide-ranging activities, including final project reviews live from all the participating universities at the same time.

New advances and innovations in the realm of online publishing are occurring so fast that it is virtually impossible to keep informed about all of them; programs in the

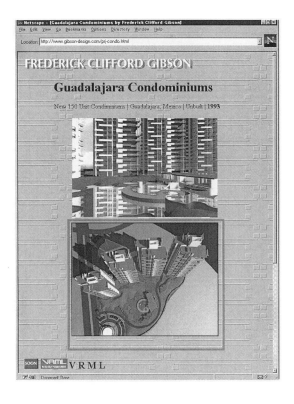

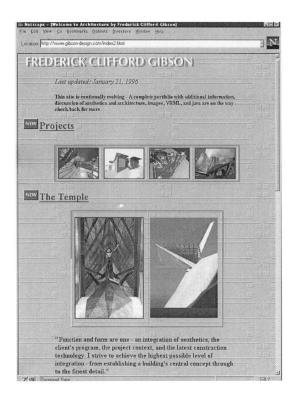

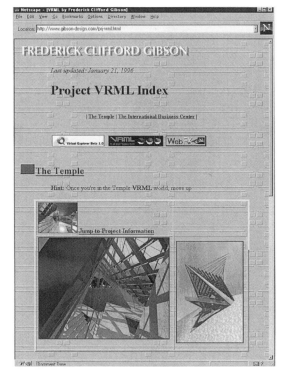

A series of web pages showing architectural design concepts from the portolio of Frederick C. Gibson.

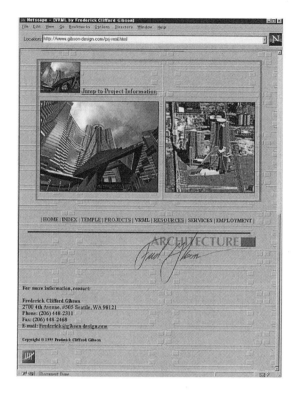

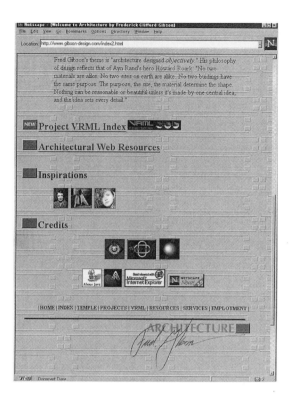

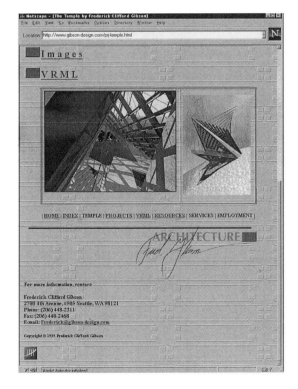

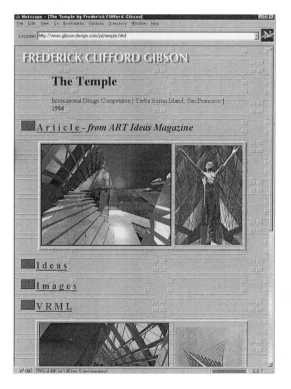

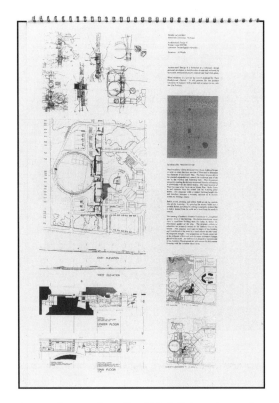

A sample page from Paul Matelic's undergraduate portfolio, a traditional approach to page design with images and text cut and pasted together and reproduced by photostatting. Paul Matelic, Massachusetts Institute of Technology, Cambridge MA. 11" x 17"

developmental stage today will be operational tomorrow and superseded the day after. For those interested in internet authorship and design, the possibilities are tremendous.

Software for creating and altering digital images is a new tool for architects and those in the allied fields of landscape design, interior architecture, and environmental and urban design. Many now use Computer-Aided Design, or CAD, to create complex two-dimensional and three-dimensional digital models, which can be altered, rotated to new perspectives, or even "entered" as if they were real structures and viewed from different points of view. "Snapshots" can be taken from any view and stored separately in another file. Among the programs for this kind of work are Autodesk AutoCAD™, Graphisoft ArchiCAD™, Engineered Software Power CADD™, Catiea™, FormZ™, Bentley/Intergraph MicroStation™, and Strata StudioPro™.

Applications such as Adobe Photoshop™ and Adobe Photostyler™ allow you to easily change and correct digital images or alter them to produce new images. You can sharpen out-of-focus images, adjust contrast and brightness, crop images, and condense, expand, reverse, invert, or distort them. You can blend, tint, lighten, darken colors, all in a matter of seconds.

With illustration programs such as Adobe Illustrator™, MacroMedia Freehand™, and CorelDRAW™ you can create a two-dimensional design within which you can draw,

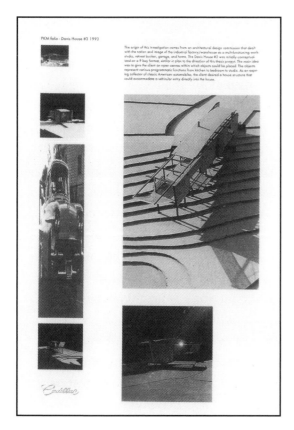

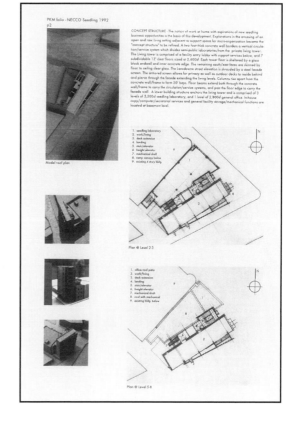

These portfolio pages were produced on a
Macintosh and test-printed on an HP 650c
printer. Many different imaging techniques
were used, yielding halftones (photographs),
line art, and type in a seamless layout.
Paul Matelic, Massachusetts Institute of
Technology, Cambridge MA. 11" x 17"

sketch, place text, create and alter shapes,
and import stored digital images. Pressure-
sensitive digital pens used on tablets respond
to variations in pressure, angle, and edge,
and can simulate actual drawing. You can
produce line art, watercolor, gouache, and
other media, and use filters to change their
transparency, shading, or tinting and add
other effects such as pattern, pointillism or
embossing. Filters for lighting effects simulate solar flares or the appearance of multiple
light sources of different colors, intensities,
and angles.

   With the latest versions of word processing
programs such as Microsoft Word™ and

WordPerfect™ and a modest supply of type fonts—either the basic sets supplied with the program or additional faces chosen from the hundreds that are readily available, you can create your text in multiple columns of varying width. Features such as Object Linking and Embedding (OLE) allow you to import almost any image that can be scanned into a digital file into these text columns, and the text will automatically flow around it.

Finally, you can combine text and images in QuarkXPress™ or Aldus PageMaker,™ widely used page layout programs that provide a broad array of layout possibilities.

Paul Matelic's undergraduate portfolio (page 122) was created through traditional photographic methods and cut and paste design. During the course of his Masters work he used his computer to create an employment portfolio. As the illustrations on page 123 demonstrate, the overall appearance is of a well-designed portfolio produced by conventional methods.

Christopher Garrison produced his portfolio entirely on a computer, including images created in AutoCAD and three-dimensional modeling (opposite). Again, perspective and viewpoint have been manipulated, as well as light and shadow. Boldly colored images such as those shown on page 96 are striking examples of the kinds of images that can be created by virtual reality systems.

Another portfolio produced on computer is that of Scott Erdy (page 126).

Aaron Adolph's landscape architecture portfolio (page 127) contains an AutoCAD

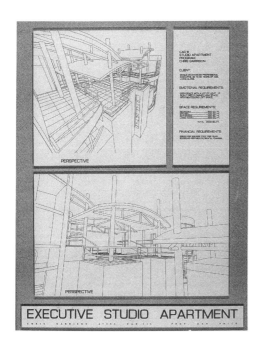

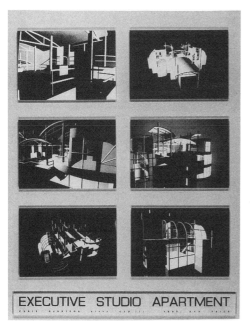

This student used AutoCAD™ and three-dimensional modeling programs. Christopher Michael Garrison, Lawrence Technological University, Southfield MI.

slide show on a floppy disk that supplements, but can be viewed independently from, the graphic presentation. The portfolio includes a mini-brochure, a resume, and the computer diskette.

The advantage of a portfolio on disk or CD is that it can be easily and economically shipped to a prospective employer, and it can be easily duplicated. Remember, however, that many professionals prefer to see actual printed pieces of your work, even if a computer disk is included. Time is of the essence

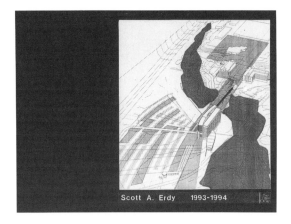

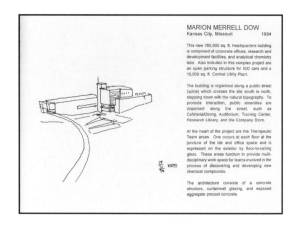

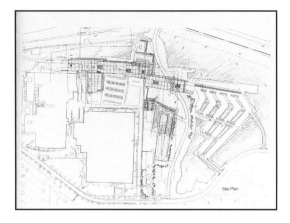

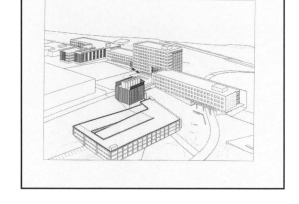

A series of pages from portfolios produced with
AutoCAD™.
Scott A. Erdy, The Hillier Group, Princeton NJ.
11" x 8 1/2"

to professionals, and they may not want to
take the time to view your digital work on a
monitor.

Many architectural firms have made big
investments in sophisticated computer systems, and many of them produce promotional
material electronically. Nevertheless, professionals feel that the technology is still in an
early stage of evolution, at least concerning
the reproduction of images with a resolution
comparable to photography and printing
processes. There are other limitations as well,

A multimedia portfolio that includes a floppy disk and hardcopy presentation.
Aaron Adolph, Louisiana State University, Baton Rouge LA.

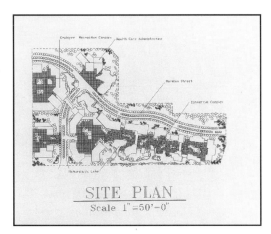

including screen size and problems in software compatibility from office to office. So think of the computer as a tool and an aid for producing flat, graphic designs of the traditional type. But you need to acquire computer skills and become proficient. Experiment with designing a portfolio for the World Wide Web. Eventually, the digital portfolio will become fully accepted, but for now a "physical" record of your work is still preferable to a virtual record.

This professional portfolio from a design office contains individual, interchangeable pages showing the firm's projects. Many design firms use this kind of modular system, which allows them to include a selection of relevant pieces in a portfolio submitted for a particular job.
Barry Ridge Graphic Design, Westlake Village CA. 6" x 9"

Another office brochure system with double-folded pieces selected to suit individual clients.
SDI-HTI, New York NY. 8 1/2" x 11"

When they called you crybaby
or poor or fat or crazy
and made you into an alien.

5.
A Portfolio
of Portfolios

A black background gives dramatic contrast
to a collage from a plate portfolio.
Jillian V. Lustig, Art Center College of Design,
Pasadena CA. 10″ x 13″

Believing in the effectiveness of learning
by example, I present in this chapter a variety of portfolios that embody novel or interesting solutions to questions of page
structure, image presentation, and sequencing. You may find here a solution to your own
design problem, or you may simply note a
style or method to keep in mind for the future. In addition to looking at other people's
portfolios, remember to stay abreast of design
trends by making frequent trips to the library,
reading contemporary journals, and talking
to colleagues.

There are no rules set in concrete for portfolio design. The standards set by every port-

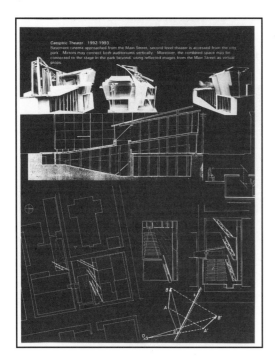

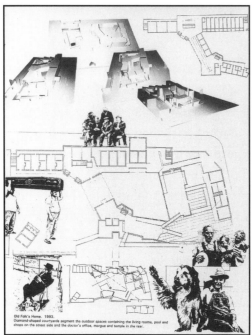

Pages that incorporate intriguing collages and
photographs for dramatic impact.
Mark Morris, The Ohio State University,
Columbus OH. 8 1/2" x 11"

folio shown here, and every guideline and
caution detailed in the preceding pages, can
be overturned if you feel compelled to do so
by the nature of the material you are presenting. That is exactly how new ideas become
old principles. But relatively inexperienced
designers should proceed cautiously.
Originality is important, but trying too hard
to be original often leads the inexperienced
designer away from commonly accepted
principles of communication, and if you cannot make your ideas clear to other individuals, your originality will be applied to no
purpose. There is enormous scope in portfolio
design for original ideas, and reviewers will
appreciate a bold leap of imagination, but
they will also be looking for creativity tem-
pered by a mature and realistic outlook.
Never forget that most professional offices
undertake projects as a team, and you will
want to demonstrate that your boldness is not
arrogance, that you possess discipline, and
that you can function as a team player.

No matter how good your portfolio is, it will
inevitably mean different things to different
people. A design firm will react differently to
your work than would an architectural engineering firm or a planning office. This is why
it is so important to research the type of company you are planning to interview with, and
if possible, to gear your presentation toward
their interests. It's a good idea to let someone
else review your finished portfolio before
presenting it to a prospective employer. You

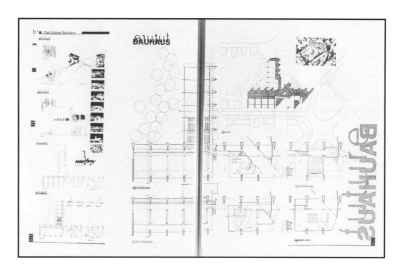

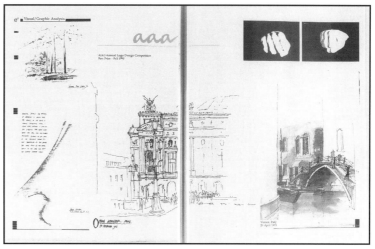

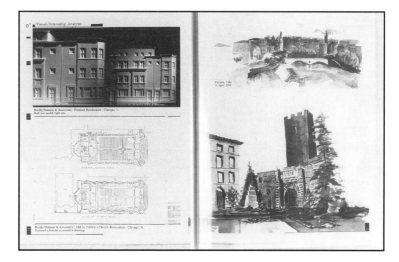

These layouts make excellent use
of double-page spreads to give
the drawings enough room for the
fine qualities of line and shade to
be seen.
Jesse Wu, University of Illinois,
Champaign-Urbana IL.
8 1/2" x 11"

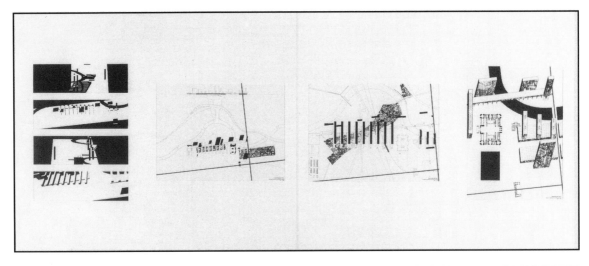

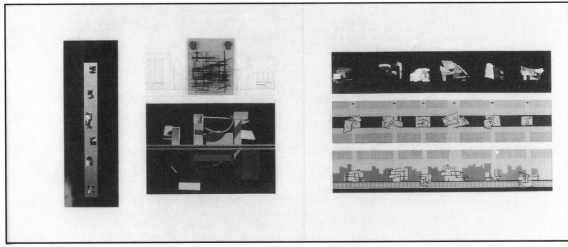

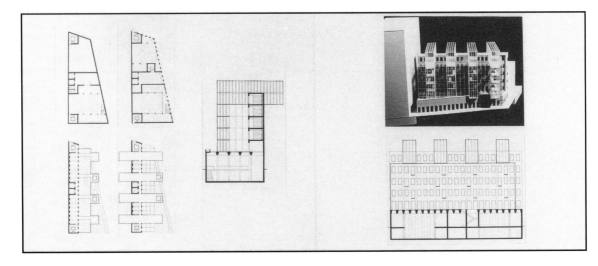

Hinged pages constructed from cardstock in a hand-crafted case covered in black canvas by a book bindery.
Rachael Eberts, Parsons School of Design, New York NY. 11" x 8 1/2"

want to know if something in your portfolio doesn't make sense or lacks an adequate explanation. Go over your portfolio yourself as objectively as possible, reviewing every element and how it works in conjunction with other elements. Ask yourself these basic questions: Is the portfolio well organized? Does it clearly illustrate your strengths and technical abilities as a designer? Does it show how your ideas develop and how you solve problems? Does it present a focused vision? Review the overall layout, the photography, the typography, and the reproduction methods. Are the pages in mint condition or have they become dog-eared after frequent reviews? Are the images presented sharply and clearly, with adequate contrast? Are the projects included up to date, reflecting your best and most recent work? Do the views of your work make sense, and do subsequent pages expand upon and make clearer the previous pages? Is the photography sharp and clear, and is the text legible? Will the reviewer understand the material without having you present to explain the portfolio?

Once your portfolio has won you an interview, what can you expect? A typical interview lasts a half-hour or more, and is normally conducted by a member of the faculty or administration or, in a professional office, by a member of the design team, a partner, project manager, or personnel officer. You will be asked questions about your education, your previous employment and the projects you have completed, as well as, perhaps, a number of personal questions

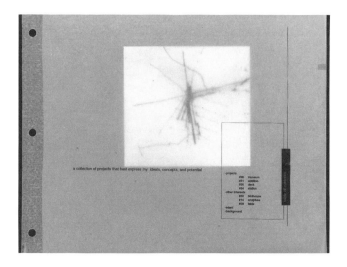

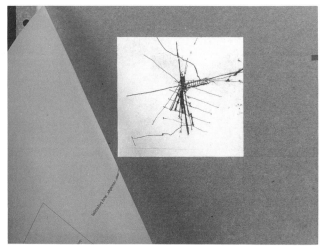

Overlays, ample text, and clear drawings,
mounted on textured paper.
Paul John Boulifard, North Carolina State
University, Raleigh NC. 11″ x 8 1/2″

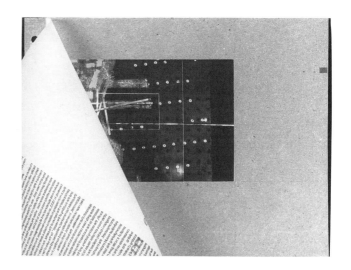

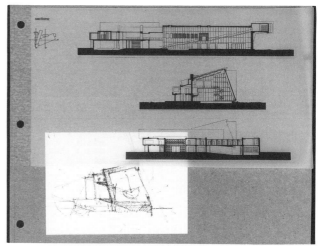

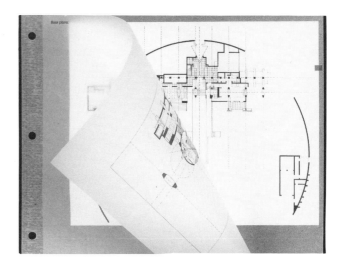

about your goals. Not everything the interviewer wants to know may be formally solicited through a question, but in general conversation you will reveal much about your personal interests and goals. Almost certainly, you will be asked why you chose your field of study and how you see yourself fitting into the school or firm. Know your portfolio and the projects in it well, and be prepared to talk about them. Learn from the experience if the reviewer is confused about some aspect of your presentation, and fix the problem before your next interview.

It is also important to come to the interview with some carefully prepared questions of your own. Unless you demonstrate interest and curiosity about the company and your position within it, the interview is not likely to be interesting for either party. You will want to know how the office is structured and how design teams operate, the prospects for advancement, and of course before you arrive you will have learned something about the kind of work they do—commercial, residential, or institutional. Certainly, it is not the only interview you have scheduled, nor is this the only firm you are prepared to work for, but interest in the company and eagerness to learn more are always appreciated. Remember that the interviewer wants to know what you can do for the company, not what it can do for you.

In preparing your portfolio, you must balance two functions. The portfolio is a creative act, showing your skills and imagination, but it is also an act of communication and a tool

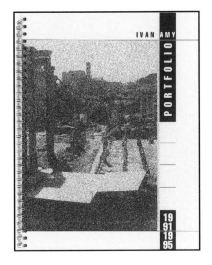

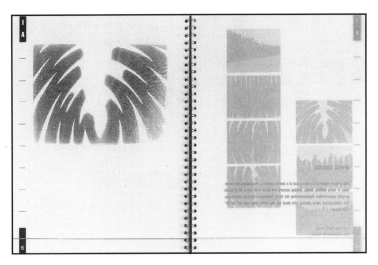

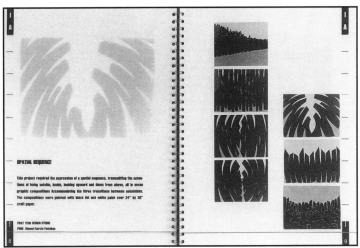

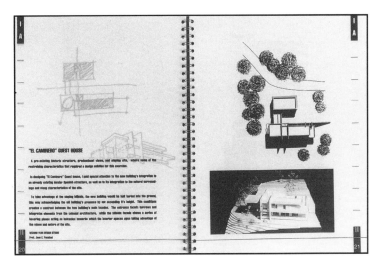

A very graphic approach, with strong
type balancing a variety of images.
Ivan Amy, Escuela de Arquitectura,
University of Puerto Rico, San Juan
PR. 8 1/2″ x 11″

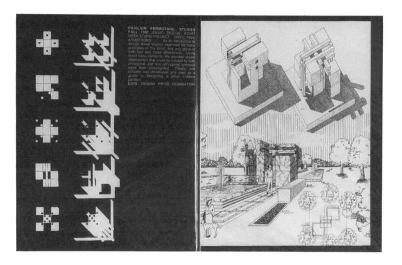

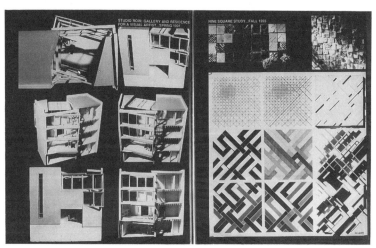

Multiple images organized in a
carefully paced sequence of
graphic elements with a black
background that heightens their
impact.
Christine McGrath, University of
Illinois, Champaign-Urbana IL.
8 1/2" x 11"

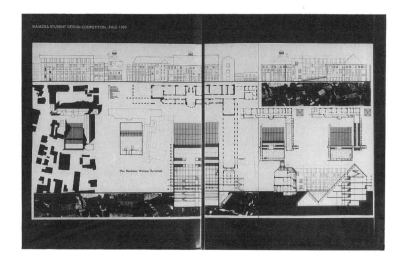

for self-promotion. Demonstrate originality and inventiveness, but also accept the restrictions and conventions of professionalism, and show that you can get your ideas across in terms that working architects and designers can understand. Such a balance between creativity and practicality should come naturally to you. In the crudest terms, a building may be flamboyantly original, but it must not fall down. Interior architecture must be functional. Landscaping must be appropriate. The design of a portfolio may break all the rules, but it must be clear and comprehensible to the viewer by creating its own rules. The struggle between inventiveness and formality is one that will be with you for your entire career as a designer, and the portfolio presentation is where both concepts have to come together naturally, for this is where you tell others what you are capable of doing in your chosen field.

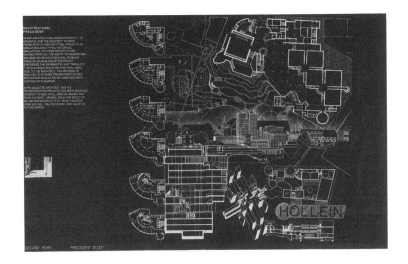

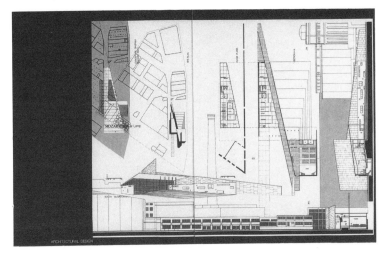

The images extend over three-quarters of a double-page spread, with space for a single column of text on the left-hand page.
Anthony Montalto, University of Illinois, Champaign-Urbana IL.
8 1/2″ x 11″

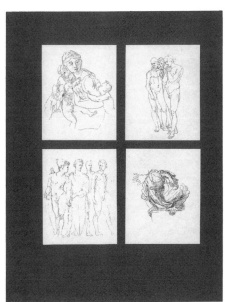

A boxed set of plates in a handmade case of black mat board with Velcro tab.
The type and visuals are carefully arranged and laminated on black boards,
with sections clearly demarcated by dividers.
Jillian V. Lustig, Art Center College of Design, Pasadena CA. 10″ x 13″

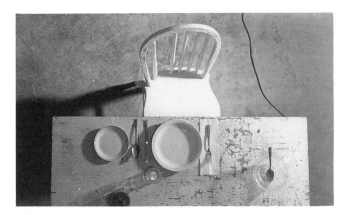

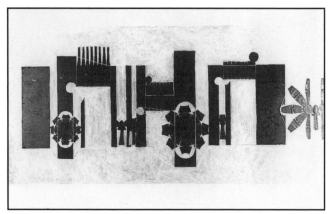

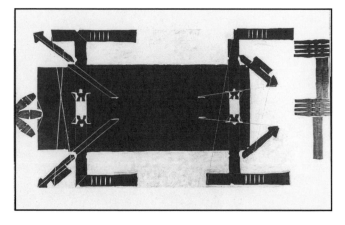

An unusual portfolio by a graduate in architecture, these pages explore topological views of a table and chair with latex rubber and the possibilities of layering the medium into continuous developed surfaces. The studies reflect surface depiction of texture and material processes.
Jeanine Centuori, Architecture Studio, Cranbrook Academy of Art, Bloomfield Hills MI. 10″ x 13″

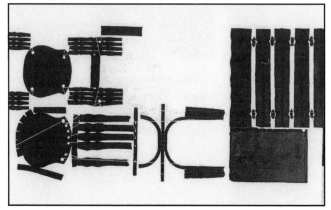

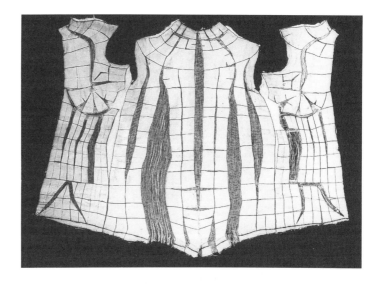

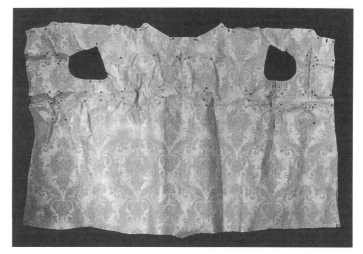

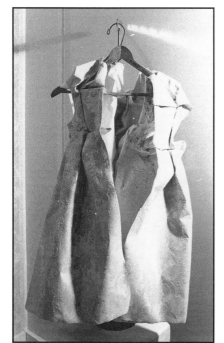

This study in definition of planar surfaces explores the potential of layering and unfolding form for a graduate thesis project. Through the operation of the fold, a flat continuous surface can be developed into a three-dimensional form integrating the nature of a wall plane with aspects of human form.
Monica Wyatt, Architecture Studio, Cranbrook Academy of Art, Bloomfield Hills MI. 10″ x 8″

Another portfolio with no explicitly architectural subject matter, this is an exploration of a 1935 Burroughs typewriter to find new forms, meanings, and processes within the component parts. Artistic innovation is evident in the assemblage of resin-coated transparent panels shown in the studio and in photographic prints.
Jonathan Rader
Architecture Studio, Cranbrook Academy of Art, Bloomfield Hills MI.

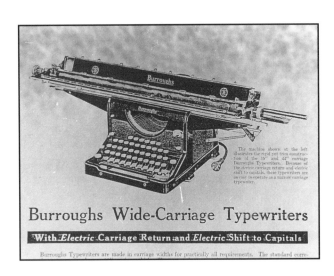

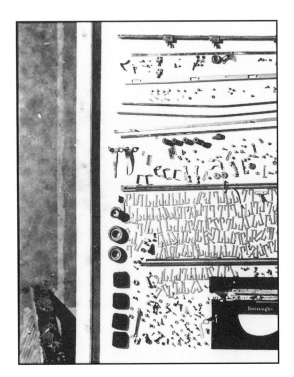

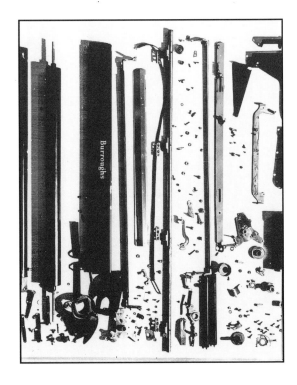

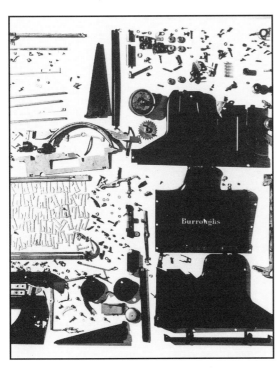

SELECTED
BIBLIOGRAPHY

Berryman, Greg. *Designing Creative Portfolios*. Menlo Park, California: Crisp, 1994.

———.*Designing Creative Resumes*. Menlo Park, California: Crisp, 1991.

———. *Notes on Graphic Design and Visual Communication*. Los Altos, California: William Kaufmann, 1979.

Biesele, Igildo G. *Graphic Design Education*. New York: Hastings House, 1981.

Brackman, Henrietta. *The Perfect Portfolio*. New York: Watson-Guptill, 1984.

Craig, James. *Designing with Type*. New York: Watson-Guptill: 1980.

Foote, Cameron. *The Business Side of Creativity*. New York: W.W. Norton, 1996.

Gray, Bill. Revised by Paul Shaw. *Studio Tips for Artists and Graphic Designers*. New York: W.W. Norton, 1996.

———. *Tips on Type*. New York: W.W. Norton, 1996.

Hofman, Armin. *Graphic Design Manual*. New York: Van Nostrand Reinhold, 1965.

Marquand, Ed. *How to Prepare Your Portfolio*. New York: Art Direction, 1985.

Metzdorf, Martha. *The Ultimate Portfolio*. Cincinnati: North Light Books, 1991.

Resnick, Elizabeth. *Graphic Design: A Problem-Solving Approach to Visual Communication*. Englewood Cliffs, NJ: Prentice-Hall, 1984.

Scher, Paula. *The Graphic Design Portfolio*. Watson-Guptill, New York, 1992.

White, Jan V. *Graphic Idea Notebook*. New York: Watson-Guptill, 1980.

INDEX

Page numbers in italics refer to illustrations.

148